The internet and information skills

a guide for teachers and school librarians

The internet and information skills
a guide for teachers and school librarians

James E. Herring

facet publishing

© James E. Herring 2004

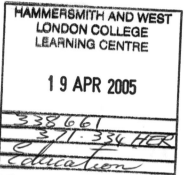

Published by
Facet Publishing
7 Ridgmount Street
London WC1E 7AE

Facet Publishing (formerly Library Association Publishing) is wholly owned by CILIP: the Chartered Institute of Library and Information Professionals.

First published 2004

British Library Cataloguing in Publication Data
A catalogue record for this book is available from the British Library.

ISBN 1-85604-493-9

Typeset in 11/14 pt Elegant Garamond and Geometric 415 by Facet Publishing Production.
Printed and made in Great Britain by MPG Books Ltd, Bodmin, Cornwall.

This book is dedicated to my two
handsome and warm-hearted sons

Jonathan Ian Herring
and
Stuart James Herring

Contents

Acknowledgements

I would like to thank all the teachers, school librarians, teacher librarians and library media specialists who have sent me material for this book. As always, I have had to be selective in my choice of material mainly because of demands on space but I hope that my selection will be useful to readers. In particular, I would like to thank the following people for their material and advice: Anne-Marie Tarter, Maggie Ashcroft, Simon Sykes, Chris Morrison, Barbara Lee, Lynn Barrett, Ken Lovett, Alle Goldsworthy, Rosalind Kentwell, Joyce Valenza, Lyn Hay, Debbie Abilock, Linda Hughes, Maureen Carter, Jim Sharp, Nahad Gilbert, Kelly Smith, Judith Sprawling, Eileen Armstrong, Jamie McKenzie, Janet Murray, Dale Duffin, Faye Baxter, Ian Prior, Tom March, Moira Ekdahl, Tom Kaun, Richard Jarrald, Elizabeth Derouet, Hugh Eveleigh, John Landells and John Hannan.

Thanks must also go to Rebecca Casey and Lin Franklin at Facet Publishing for their helpful advice and editing.

Finally, love and thanks to my wife Val for patiently suffering the book writing process once more.

Introduction: the internet and the need for effective information skills

The purpose of this book

The internet is now available both in primary/elementary and in secondary/high schools in most parts of the world, but access to it remains very limited in some countries. In developed countries, however, the internet is now accessible not only in school libraries but also in classrooms and computer rooms. In the past five years, the number of computers in schools has risen dramatically so that access to the internet is now provided mostly via the school's network or intranet, rather than via a modem in its library's computer.

The purposes of this book are, first, to provide teachers and school librarians[1] across the world with a theoretical context and a practical guide to effective exploitation of different aspects of the internet for educational purposes. As a consequence of recent developments in learning and teaching in schools, teachers are being encouraged (and trained) to use ICT to develop more innovative teaching methods and students[2] are not merely encouraged but often *required* to use both print and electronic information resources when completing school work, especially assignments.

In today's schools, learning from the teacher alone is being replaced, to some extent, by learning from both the teacher and from information resources. Given this context, the need for students to be effective users of information becomes paramount along with the need for students to be *taught* how to become effective users of information (in whatever form). Thus, a second purpose of this book is to update teachers' and school librarians' knowledge of information skills and information literacy, particularly in relation to their own and their students' use of the internet and the world wide web in particular.

The third purpose of this book emerges from its context: teachers and school librarians are constantly seeking help and advice on how to exploit the internet effectively as both a learning and a teaching resource. In particular, teachers and school librarians are looking for ways to improve their knowledge in accessing the most *relevant* parts of the internet in order to improve their teaching or to provide students with suitable information sources which can aid their learning. Both teachers and school librarians recognize that information literacy is one of the key skills needed by today's students (who are tomorrow's workers in the knowledge economy) and they are also constantly seeking help and advice on the most effective ways of teaching them information skills. This book aims to provide that help and advice by providing teachers and school librarians with a mixture of theory and best practice.

The book begins by providing teachers and school librarians with an examination of current theories about the learning and teaching context of the internet in schools and the importance of teaching information skills. This is followed by Chapters 2, 3 and 4, which cover the internet, evaluating websites, and subject gateways, giving teachers and school librarians up-to-date advice on current developments, e.g. using search engines to find curriculum-related material (which can either extend the teacher's knowledge or be potentially useful for students); evaluating the content of websites for both teaching and learning purposes; and using subject gateways to find teaching and learning materials designed or evaluated by other teachers and school librarians.

Chapters 5 and 6 focus on information skills and student use of the web, providing teachers and school librarians with an update on information literacy and information skills models, and also including an outline of the author's PLUS model and how it can be used to improve students' use of the web. These two chapters contain a range of examples from schools around the world, which teachers and school librarians may put to practical use by adapting them for their own schools. The examples of in-service training in relation to information skills and the web are based on sessions that the author has designed and delivered, both in the UK and in other countries.

Chapters 7 and 8 give teachers and school librarians a practical guide to developing school websites and instructional websites, using a range of international examples. The purpose of these chapters is to encourage educators in schools to work collaboratively to produce their own school website with a *curricular* focus, to include student access to instructional websites that contain not only curriculum content but also guidance on information skills for students. These will use pre-evaluated websites as well as other resources, e.g. CD-ROMs, books and newspapers. The examples show how a combination of the teacher's subject knowledge and the school librarian's knowledge of relevant information sources can ensure that the school uses instructional websites that are effective learning tools for students. A guide to web design skills is also included.

Finally, Chapter 9 looks at future developments in the use of the internet and information skills for learning and teaching, and considers the likely effect on the roles of the teacher and the school librarian.

Who should read this book?

The main focus of the book is on secondary/high schools worldwide, but it will also be of use to those in school management, to teachers and school librarians in primary/elementary schools and to those in further education. School managers will benefit from the chapters on learning and teaching as well as from those on information skills and website development. Teachers will benefit from the ideas and examples on teaching information skills and how to ensure that their students have the requisite skills to use web resources effectively. School librarians will benefit from the ideas and examples concerning their own role in teaching information skills as well as in the development of the library website and their potential role in collaborating with teachers in designing instructional websites. The book should also be on the reading lists for trainee teachers and school librarians in the UK, USA, Canada, Australia and South Africa, so that they can be prepared to implement some of the ideas and examples in the book when they become professional educators.

Notes

1 The term 'school librarian' is used throughout this book to cover professionally qualified librarians working in schools around the world. The term covers, for example, school librarians in the UK, as well as teacher–librarians in Australia and Canada and library media specialists in the USA who have dual qualifications in teaching and librarianship/information management.
2 The term 'student' is used throughout this book to denote young people attending primary/elementary or secondary/high schools in different countries. It is recognized that some schools still use the term 'pupils'.

1

The learning and teaching context

....

Having read this chapter, you will:

* be familiar with current theories on learning and, in particular, individual learning
* view information skills in the context of learning in schools
* understand the contribution which use of the internet can make to student learning in schools
* be up to date with the theories and practices of effective teaching
* be able to identify and apply appropriate teaching styles that can be used in the classroom and the school library
* understand the potential use of the internet as a resource for teaching and the benefits of teacher/school librarian collaboration.

....

Introduction

As the use of the internet in schools is growing, along with the pressure on teachers and school librarians to use it for curricular purposes, it is important to consider the key reasons for arguing that the internet, and in particular the world wide web, should be an important resource for use in the school curriculum. The motivation for using the web as a resource for students and staff should be based on *educational* criteria, i.e. to improve both learning and teaching in a school and not merely because of its technological availability. Use of the web in the school library, classroom or ICT lab should not be an example of technological determinism, where the main reason for using a new technology is its existence: *because* it exists, it *must* be used. If the web is used in a school in this way, the use is likely to be very superficial and the links to curricular work peripheral. Thus, if students' only experience of using the web is an exercise in an ICT lab, learning to use the Google search engine but allowed to search for random topics, they are unlikely to see the potential benefits of the web as a learning resource. Instead, it may be seen merely as a recreational tool. School management staff, teachers and school librarians all need to examine the key issues in both learning and teaching in schools and then to assess the extent to which using the internet – e-mail and the web – can support and improve learning and teaching in the school. This chapter will seek to examine relevant learning theories, effective learners, concept mapping, and learning and the internet as well as effective teaching, teaching styles, and teaching and the internet.

Learning
Learning theories

Learning is a very complicated process and no two learners learn in *exactly* the same way. Furthermore, there is no single theory of learning that is universally accepted and put into practice in schools. Therefore, teachers and school librarians will benefit from a knowledge of some definitions of learning and the key elements of some major learning theories, as it will help them to guide their students as developing learners in the school. Lieberman (1999) provides a definition of learning as 'a change in our *capacity* for behaviour, as a result of particular *kinds* of experience', and Schunk (2000) argues that: 'Learning is an enduring change in behaviour, or in the capacity to behave in a given fashion, which results from practice or other forms of experience.'

Learning in schools can be seen as a process in which students develop knowledge and skills via the experiences referred to in these definitions. In order for students to learn effectively, teachers and school librarians need to provide the students with the right kinds of learning experiences so that the students become effective learners (see below) and acquire new knowledge and skills.

Behaviourist theories

The key learning theories which were popular in the first half of the 20th century were behaviourist theories. While behaviourist theories are no longer seen as of key importance to the curriculum of the 21st century, certain elements of the theories are recognized as still being useful. According to Schunk (2000), behaviourist theories stress that learning is the association between stimuli and response and the reinforcement of skills, but are best suited to simpler forms of learning such as learning to count or acquiring facts. Skinner, the leading behaviourist, argued that children's learning can be shaped and that their learning behaviour can be changed via repetition of tasks and reinforcement. However, Schunk criticizes this approach and states that 'by ignoring mental process, operant conditioning [Skinner's approach] offers an incomplete account of human learning'.

Schunk also states that while behavioural principles can be applied in some areas of the curriculum, they are not appropriate where deeper learning is required.

Behaviourist theories can also be seen in relation to what Carnell and Lodge (2002) state as the 'reception model' of learning. In this model, Carnell and Lodge argue that 'the learner is a passive recipient of knowledge which is transmitted by the teacher' and that learners are concerned mainly with knowledge acquisition and the ability to memorize and produce evidence of what knowledge has been acquired. In this model, learners are concerned more with how much they can learn as opposed to the quality of what they learn. This approach is problematic, according to Carnell and Lodge, as it may make the learner too dependent on the teacher. It may also be seen as a restricted approach where students have little choice in terms of assessment and any feedback they are given will tend to be evaluative, expressed in terms of *what* they have learned as opposed to *how well* they have learned. If teachers and school librarians adopt the reception model of learning, Carnell and Lodge argue that students will not benefit as learners: 'The reception model of learning does not encourage selectivity and judgement about what it is important to know. It does not encourage transfer of learning to different contexts and it fails to address the learner's understanding of themselves as a learner.'

In relation to information skills and the use of the internet, a behaviourist approach or reception model approach to learning would be very restrictive. Students might be taught the technical aspects of using a search engine to find information but would tend to focus on the quantity of information found as opposed to its quality, and there would be little encouragement for them either to evaluate the information or to examine their approach to finding relevant information. Loertscher and Woolls (2002) state that when students are taught in classrooms where behavioural approaches to learning are employed, they often find using a school library problematic because the teacher may then expect them to adopt an inquiry mode of learning, which they find themselves ill-equipped to do.

Cognitive theories

Schunk (2000) argues that more attention must be paid to students' cognitive processes in relation to learning. Cognitive approaches to learning tend to focus more on the learners as individuals and on the learners taking more responsibility for their learning, with the teacher or school librarian as someone who can organize meaningful activities for students. These 'meaningful activities' will tend to relate more to problem solving or hypothesis testing than to the mere acquisition of information about a topic. Thus, if year 7 (11 to 12 year old) students were studying aspects of earthquakes in geography, it would benefit them more to use the web to find information on earthquakes in relation to particular questions, such as 'Why do earthquakes occur?' rather than just to find as much information as possible on earthquakes.

Bloom's Taxonomy

One example of a cognitive theory that encourages students to be more independent learners is Bloom's Taxonomy of Learning. Thomas (1999) states that Bloom viewed learning in relation to the difficulty of tasks; his Taxonomy identified skills which grew in complexity according to the demand made on the students' cognitive ability. In the Taxonomy, level 1 is recognition, i.e. basic skills such as the ability to put names to objects and people and remember them, whereas level 4 is application, which is a more sophisticated learning skill such as the ability to manipulate existing knowledge to facilitate new learning. Other key elements of the Taxonomy include synthesis (level 6), the ability to create new knowledge by collecting a range of ideas and facts, and evaluation (level 7), the ability to judge the value or quality of ideas or activities.

In relation to information skills, Bloom's Taxonomy of Learning is a very apt model for teachers and school librarians because the focus is on developing the student's ability to be a critical thinker. Schools using a model of information skills such as PLUS are demanding that students show abilities in the upper levels of Bloom's Taxonomy: in the PLUS model, the final stage of self-evaluation takes Bloom's level further in that students are asked to evaluate their own abilities. In relation to the use of the web, Bloom's Taxonomy is also relevant in that teachers and school librarians will wish their students not merely to be able to retrieve information (level 2) but also to be able to retrieve information and ideas according to a planned strategy, to relate what they find to existing knowledge and to evaluate the quality of ideas and information which they find (levels 6 and 7).

Constructivism

The increased use of ICT and the internet in schools across the world has alerted educators to the need to pay more attention to students' learning skills. This has renewed interest in constructivist ideas in education as constructivism places more emphasis on the need for students to become more active participants in their own learning rather than being seen to be passive learners who wait to receive knowledge from the teacher. Schunk (2000) argues that constructivism 'postulates that knowledge is not acquired automatically but rather that learners construct their own understandings,' and that 'constructivism calls our attention to the fact that we must structure teaching and learning experiences so that students' thinking will be challenged sufficiently so that they will be able to construct new knowledge'.

The emphasis in constructivism therefore is on learners who are active and who gain new knowledge not just from the teacher but through asking questions and finding answers by independently using a range of information sources, from books to the internet to people in their own community or family. Schunk argues that constructivists may be open to criticism if they argue that students can learn effectively without having some guidance from teachers, stating that 'The extent of student learning is dependent on both student capabilities in developing knowledge from group discussions and teacher skills in establishing thoughtful and reflective dialogue.'

Carnell and Lodge (2002) state that constructivism is a useful model of learning that encourages students to think more about their own learning and 'what it is important to know'. They criticize the model by stating that it may stress individual aspects of learning too much and that 'future learners' will need more skills related to learning as part of a team. Carnell and Lodge argue that what they term the 'co-constructivist model' is more relevant to today's schools as it places more emphasis on dialogue between students and that some of the advantages of dialogue are that students can be *'engaged* in conversation in a spontaneous way' and *'open* to new ideas and ways of thinking'. A recent study by Herring et al. (2002) focused partly on year 7 (11 to 12 year-old) students' opinions on brainstorming; the findings concurred with those of Carnell and Lodge, i.e. students enjoyed brainstorming because of the dialogue engaged and the ideas generated through open discussion.

Constructivist approaches to learning have become more fashionable in recent years with the increased stress on enabling students to become more independent learners and have less reliance on the teacher. In reality, student learning in today's schools is the result of a range of approaches, from the behaviourist approach in introducing students to new areas of study to more constructivist approaches where students are allowed to explore new topics on their own or as part of a group.

For teachers and school librarians who are teaching information skills so that students may use print and electronic information resources more effectively, it is likely that a more constructivist approach will be more fruitful but it should be remembered that students will still need much guidance in developing as independent learners and will not learn effectively if they are, for example, allowed to use search engines to explore new topics without adequate guidance about planning a search strategy.

Matusevich (1995) provides examples from Montgomery Schools which took a constructivist approach and states that there was increasing evidence of 'cooperative learning where students naturally collaborate on projects', and that the schools viewed 'students as active learners' and the 'teacher as facilitator'. In these schools, students took part in 'authentic activities' involving 'higher level thinking skills' and 'self evaluation'. By examining such approaches, teachers and school librarians can adapt their own approach to encouraging active learning among students.

Effective learners

In schools that encourage students to be more independent learners, there is now much attention paid to methods which will make students 'effective learners' not only in school but in employment, in future education and as lifelong learners. Carnell and Lodge (2002) cite research which states that the results of effective learning should include 'higher order skills and strategies', 'enhanced sense of self', 'further learning strategies' and 'greater affiliation to learning'.

The authors argue that they are keen to encourage schools to concentrate on four key elements of learning:

• active learning
• collaborative learning
• responsible learning
• meta-learning, i.e. learning about learning.

In teaching information skills to students, teachers and school librarians are following the guidance provided by Carnell and Lodge and others: if students are provided with the requisite information skills to exploit information resources, this will help them to become effective learners. Students will be *active* in seeking relevant information and ideas from books and the web; *collaborative* in activities such as the brainstorming of topics; *responsible* in planning search strategies and seeking only information relevant to their purpose; and will become *meta-learners*, able to reflect on their approach to learning and seek improvement in their use of information resources and the products of their research, e.g. assignments.

Concept mapping

Learning theories' emphasis on students reflecting on their existing knowledge has led to extensive use of concept mapping as an activity which encourages both active and (when linked with brainstorming) collaborative learning. A concept map is a visual representation of information which could otherwise be represented textually. Thus this chapter has so far examined aspects of learning, including:

• behaviourism
• Bloom's Taxonomy
• constructivism
• effective learners
• concept mapping.

However, this list could also be represented visually as in Figure 1.1.

It should be noted here that neither the list nor the concept map actually shows the relationships between the different elements of learning apart from

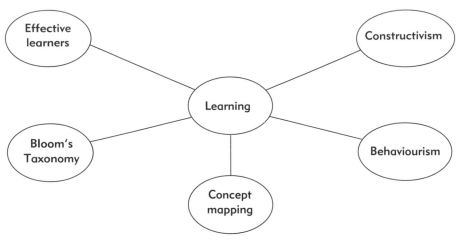

Figure 1.1   Concept map

the fact that each of the elements can be seen as a subsection of learning. However, Hyerle (2000) argues that 'brainstorming webs' or concept maps should not be seen as 'a static visual picture … that is somewhat disconnected to further creative and analytical work [but as] … a running video of evolving mental models'. In the UK, Kinchin and Hay (2000) studied the use of concept maps in science classes and argue that 'concept mapping can be a helpful metacognitive tool, promoting understanding in which new material interacts with the students' existing cognitive structure'.

Kinchin and Hay also state that students' concept maps can be studied by teachers to gauge individual students' levels of understanding of ideas or topics. In a study by Herring et al. (2002), it was found that students used brainstorming and concept maps to identify existing knowledge, select topics, identify keywords', take notes and write assignments. As will be seen in subsequent chapters, the use of concept mapping in teaching information skills to students using the web as a source of information can result in more effective student learning.

Learning and the internet

Much of what is written about the internet relates either to technical aspects of internet access or to a variety of descriptions of the internet as a vast library or galaxy of information. While it is often *implied* that the internet, and particularly the web, can be a tool that will enhance student learning, there are as yet few examples of actual research evidence linking use of the internet to student learning in schools. However, there is evidence that the potential of the internet for learning is being recognized by governments and educational authorities. For example, in the UK, the Department for Education and Skills (DfES, 2003) argues that 'ICT makes a significant contribution to teaching and learning across all subjects and ages, inside and outside the curriculum', and that the internet is a key part of ICT in schools. Kent Education Authority's (2003) guidelines on internet use in schools begin with encouraging statements such as:

> Increased computer numbers or improved Internet access may be provided but effective use and quality of learning must also be addressed. Developing good practice in Internet use as a tool for teaching and learning is clearly essential. Librarians and teachers need to help pupils learn to distil the meaning from the mass of information provided by the Web.

Similarly, Sandwell Education and Lifelong Learning (2002) argue that:

> The purpose of Internet use in schools is to raise educational standards [and] to promote pupil achievement ... Internet use should be planned, task-orientated and educational within a regulated and managed environment.

Northamptonshire County Council (2000) also emphasizes the potential of the internet to contribute to learning, stating that:

> The purpose of Internet access in school is to contribute to learning and to the raising of educational standards. ... Internet access is an integral part of the use of ICT to support learning and the management of learning [and] an integral part of a large majority of schemes of work to enrich and extend learning activities.

In Canada, Gibson et al. (1999) state that using the internet as a tool to improve student learning depends on a number of factors such as the availability of hardware and software in the school, how teachers and school librarians view the internet as a new tool for learning, and 'the adoption of new models of teaching and learning'. In the USA, Slowinski argues that 'the Internet could revolutionise learning' and that using the internet effectively can allow students to 'take responsibility for their own learning'. If students are encouraged to do this, Slowinski (1999) states that students will then be engaged in learning to learn and that 'Students who know how to learn will be those who are adaptive and thus always employable.'

If using the internet in schools is to contribute to student learning, it is clear that teachers and school librarians will have to ensure that student use of the web is viewed as a normal part of the students' curricular work and not an activity which is independent of or peripheral to the students' learning activities in school, at home or in other learning centres, such as public libraries.

Teaching
Effective teaching

Effective learning on the part of students will, in part, depend on effective teaching and it is important for teachers and school librarians to review the key elements of effective teaching so that they can seek to improve their teaching in general and their teaching of information skills in particular. Kyriacou (1998) argues that 'The essence of being an effective teacher lies in knowing what to do to foster pupils' learning and being able to do it. ... Effective teaching is primarily concerned with setting up a learning activity for each pupil which is successful in bringing about the type of learning the teacher intends.'

Kyriacou also states that effective teaching is a complex mix of knowledge, skills and attitudes which is based partly on the subject knowledge of the teacher but also on skills such as flexibility and adaptability in the classroom. Effective teachers therefore, according to Kyriacou, are able to:

- create an environment which is conducive to learning and in which students feel at ease
- make the best of the time available in a lesson
- deliver lessons which are carefully structured and in which students have a clear idea of the exact purpose of the lesson
- monitor student progress and provide students with feedback which will help to improve student learning.

One of the key elements in effective teaching is, according to Tileston (2000): 'creating an enriched and emotionally supportive environment', where there is a balance between too much and too little challenge for students; where students are active learners and not totally dependent on the teacher; where teachers encourage students to produce high-quality work and support students in their efforts; and where students are viewed as individuals. In supporting this, Schunk (2000) states that students should feel that the classroom or school library where students are learning should be viewed as 'cooperative' rather than 'authoritarian' and also stresses support for students.

Tubbs (1996) argues that an effective teacher will be one who has planned sessions with students well in advance. Lesson planning, Tubbs (1996) argues, relates to basic but vital questions, including:

- Why is the lesson being taught and how does it relate to the rest of the course? Learning outcomes should be established.
- What resources will be needed for the session and are the resources available?
- When will each activity in the session take place and how long will the activity last?
- How will the teacher present the lesson to the students and will the teacher be able to employ a range of presentation styles suitable to the content of the lesson?

Figure 1.2 is an example of a lesson planning sheet which might be used by teachers and school librarians who are teaching information skills to students or incorporating use of the web into learning sessions.

Effective teaching can also be seen where teachers and school librarians are clearly in control of the learning environment. Tubbs (1996) states that: 'Control in the history of schooling has largely been associated with discipline and punishment [but] … control in the classroom is now a matter of encouragement, enablement, reward and praise.' Tubbs argues that effective teachers have the respect of students who understand what behaviour is expected of them in different situations. Schunk (2000) agrees with this and states that effective teachers criticize the *behaviour* of students, not the students themselves: criticism can be useful where it is clear to the student that the teacher has higher expectations of the student's behaviour and work. Kyriacou (1998) states that, in relation to control and discipline, the teacher in charge of the students should establish clear rules about behaviour and get the agreement of students about these rules. If the approach is collaborative between students and teacher, then misbehaviour can be pre-empted and discipline can take the form of counselling and help as well as reprimands. Kyriacou stresses the importance of avoiding confrontations with students.

Lesson Plan – Example

Theme	
Level	
Curricular Areas	
Aims	
Objectives	
Learning Outcomes	
Activities and Time-frame	
Resources Needed	
Backup Materials	
Differentiation/ Extension	
Assessment/ Evaluation	

Figure 1.2   Lesson planning sheet (copyright Robert Gordon University and Queen Margaret University College, Scotland, UK)

Teaching styles

Effective teachers will employ a range of teaching styles in the delivery of lesson content but the trend in teaching in many countries is towards a more constructivist approach to teaching. Kyriacou (1998) argues that an effective teaching style will be reflected in the presentation of the lesson and that an effective style will demonstrate that:

- the teacher is confident and the students are interested
- the teacher explains the purpose and content of the lesson clearly
- the students are actively involved in the lesson in answering questions or working independently or in groups
- the work done by students is differentiated according to the needs of students
- the students view the teacher as someone who provides challenges but also encouragement.

Loertscher and Woolls (2002) compare behaviourist with constructivist approaches, stating that where school librarians and teachers collaborate, constructivist approaches are likely to be more conducive to student learning. According to Loertscher (2000) a behaviourist teacher:

- tends to rely more on a lecture style of delivery backed by the use of textbooks
- has total control of the classroom
- takes the role of the 'sage on the stage'
- stresses the ability of students to master content
- employs assessment related to mastery of content.

Such teachers will be heavily influenced by the pressure of internal or external testing of students and Loertscher states that behaviourist teachers are often criticized because of their emphasis on content and lack of attention to the learning process.

At the other extreme, in terms of teaching style, constructivist teachers, according to Loertscher, will:

- emphasize students' use of a range of learning resources
- be facilitators of learning, as opposed to deliverers of content

- take the role of 'the guide on the side'
- involve students more in their own learning and encourage them to evaluate it.

In most schools today, while there is a move towards more involvement of students in their own learning, many teachers are reluctant to give up the relatively safe, more behaviourist style of teaching altogether and, in practice, it would not be realistic to expect them to do this. Teachers will always be expected to introduce new ideas and concepts to students and, especially at the start of lessons, may well adopt a style which is more behaviourist. The modern curriculum emphasizes a learning environment for students, whether it be the classroom, the school library or the computer room, which encourages student use of learning resources and student involvement in their own learning. Thus, while teachers and school librarians are not abandoning behaviourist styles, they are adopting more constructivist approaches.

In teaching information skills and in integrating the use of the web into student activities, teachers and school librarians can maintain a controlled environment but can allow students more opportunity to learn through the effective use of print and electronic resources. Allowing students more freedom to work independently in the classroom and in the school library should not be seen as a threat to teachers' and school librarians' control, and does not mean that lessons should not be well planned and well delivered. The key elements of effective teaching referred to above still apply to a more constructivist teaching style and it can be argued that its adoption means that a teacher or school librarian will have to be even better organized and prepared and more flexible and adaptable than a behaviourist teacher.

Teaching and the internet

Teachers and school librarians can use the internet in different ways to support and improve their teaching. In particular, the web can be used in teaching as:

- a source of information which teachers can use to add to their own subject knowledge
- a source of information which teachers can use to find examples of similar lessons taught by other teachers
- a source of material which can be used by students in class or for project work

- a method of presenting the content of a lesson including aims and objectives, student activities, materials to be used by students and, if appropriate, assessment.

Becta (2003) states that teachers who successfully integrate use of the web into their teaching:

- drew on the skills and qualities associated with good teaching in general, such as setting high expectations, intervening purposefully, involving all pupils and creating a stimulating classroom climate
- used ICT to genuinely enhance teaching and learning
- used a range of ICT applications for teaching a range of topics
- embedded ICT into the schemes of work, using and adapting national frameworks to suit individual needs
- used ICT to manage teaching, learning and assessment of the curriculum subject
- built on and extended the whole-school approach to ICT
- used ICT to create or adapt highly imaginative resources.

Thus, it is clear that the use of the web is to *enhance* teaching and build upon the fundamentals of teaching outlined above; successful teachers and school librarians will be those who can use the web for a *combination* of the uses cited above. There are many examples on the web of how teachers have used the internet in their teaching. For example, history teachers can use the Virtual Teacher Centre (2003) section on 'Integrating ICT into History' which contains case studies, reports and research relating to using the internet in history teaching.

In the USA, the Stevens Institute of Technology (2003) addresses the issue of why teachers should use the internet in teaching, outlining the following uses of the internet:

- Using the internet as a Communication Tool
- Collecting Real Time Data/Information
- Finding Unique Sources of Information
- Publishing Student Work.

This site also provides examples of collaborative projects such as The Global Water Sampling Project as an example of the internet as a communication tool.

It adds that collecting real-time data can be a learning experience for pupils and gives as an example the Musical Plates site, 'which uses real-time earthquake data from the Internet to explore the relationship between earthquakes and plate tectonics'. In relation to unique sources of information, the availability of many of the world's newspapers online is cited as a primary source of information which can be used by teachers to find information for themselves or for students to find information for project work or to improve their foreign-language skills. Using the web to publish student work is cited as a valuable way of motivating students and encouraging the exchange of student work between schools either locally or internationally.

Leu (2002) provides a very convincing argument for using the internet to improve student literacy and argues that teachers and school librarians 'must also seek instructional practices consistent with what we know about the changes taking place in literacy as the Internet and other ICT become increasingly important to our literacy lives'. Leu introduces the Internet Workshop as a method of teaching which encourages students to learn from each other about 'content information, critical literacy skills, and the new literacies of Internet technologies'. The approach taken includes the identification of a site which has content related to a current lesson and which is suitable for the reading age/abilities of the students. Teachers are then encouraged to design an activity in which students are given a range of tasks to complete and later discuss. An example of an activity can be seen in Figure 1.3.

The activity page is purposely designed to include open-ended questions that students can discuss later, when they have completed their research activity. Leu stresses that as well as learning about Japan as a curricular topic, students can also be encouraged to discuss 'critical literacy skills' such as being able to identify a site's author and any particular stance the author might take. Leu gives a number of examples of how the Internet Workshop can be used, citing the use of the web to support students reading children's literature. In this example, teachers and school librarians have used *Cyberguides* (http://sdcoe.k12.ca.us/SCORE/cyberguide.html), which contain activities that students can complete when they are reading a work of children's literature. The students can then share their views on the book with other students.

It can be argued that using the internet in teaching depends less on the available technology – or the vast amount of information available on the web – than on the skills of teachers and school librarians able to make the most of internet materials through sound teaching techniques. Both teaching methods

An activity page developed for Internet Workshop to introduce a unit on Japan

Exploring Japan

Internet researcher: _____ Date:_____

Objectives

This Internet Workshop will introduce you to our unit on Japan. You will have an opportunity to explore an important resource on the Internet for our unit. You will also learn about recent news events from Japan and learn to think more critically about what you read on the Internet. Take notes in your internet journal and share them at our workshop session.

News about Japan

1. Go to the bookmark I have set for Kids Web Japan (http://jinjapan.org./kidsweb/) and scroll down to the bottom of this page. Now click on the button Monthly News (http://jinjapan.org/kidsweb/news.html) and read several recent news stories from Japan. Choose ones of interest to you. Find out what is happening in Japan, take notes, and be ready to share them during Internet Workshop.

_____

_____

_____

Critical thinking

2. Be a detective. What clues can you find at Kids Web Japan (http://jinjapan.org/kidsweb/) to indicate that the information at this site comes from the government of Japan? Write them down and bring these clues to Internet Workshop. How did you find them? Write down the strategies you used.

_____

_____

3. If the information at this location comes from the government of Japan, how might this shape the news stories presented in Monthly News (http://www.jinjapan.org./kidsweb/news.html)? Write down your ideas and bring them to Internet Workshop.

_____

_____

Your choice

4. Visit at least one of the many other locations at Kids Web Japan. You decide where to go! Write down notes of what you discovered and share your special discoveries with all of us during Internet Workshop.

_____

_____

Evaluation rubric

8 points—You recorded important information for each item (4 x 2 = 8 points).

2 points—You effectively shared important information with us during our workshop session, helping each of us to learn about Japan.

_____

10 points—Total

Figure 1.3   Activity page using the Internet Workshop method (www.readingonline.org)

and learning outcomes can only be improved by thus incorporating aspects of the internet into the curriculum.

Collaboration between teachers and school librarians

One of the most effective ways of improving teaching in schools is to encourage collaboration between professionals in the school. Subsequent chapters include many examples demonstrating how collaboration between teachers and school librarians can be effective in teaching information skills to students. However, collaboration in relation to teaching in the classroom is also important. Loertscher (2000) argues that 'no matter how strong or excellent a teacher is, improvement can be achieved by reaching out to others for ideas of merit', and that school administrators should encourage 'common planning time' for teachers and school librarians so they can share their expertise. School librarians are experts in identifying and evaluating relevant sources of information, in both print and electronic form, which can be useful for teachers planning lessons or for use by students in class, in the school library or elsewhere. Teachers are experts in their subjects but will freely admit to *not* being experts in sourcing relevant information. The combined expertise of the teacher and the school librarian can generate new ideas for student activities such as using books and websites identified by the school librarian. For this collaboration to be successful, school librarians must effectively market their expertise in the school rather than passively wait for teachers to seek their advice. Grover et al. (2001) identify the positive outcomes of collaboration as including:

- an increase in creativity amongst teachers and learners
- the spreading of collaboration in the school as a result of successful school librarian–teacher collaboration
- the sharing of ideas between teachers, school librarians, parents and students
- an increase in communication between teachers, school librarians and school managers.

In many schools, school librarians are viewed as the 'internet experts' and sharing this expertise with teachers is a crucial role for the schools' information professionals.

Conclusion

This chapter has sought to provide teachers and school librarians with a context of learning and teaching in schools in which the teaching of information skills and the use of the internet can be seen. It is crucial that the internet and information skills are seen in relation to more effective learning and teaching and not as separate activities or sources of information which are peripheral to the school curriculum. The following chapters will examine how elements of the internet can be used by teachers, school librarians and students and how effective teaching of information skills will enable students to use the web not merely as a source of information but as a key learning tool.

References

Becta (2003) *Common Factors in Successful ICT Practice*, www.ictadvice.org.uk/index.php.

Carnell, E. and Lodge, C. (2002) *Supporting Effective Learning*, London, Paul Chapman Publishing.

Department for Education and Skills (2003) *Fulfilling the Potential*, London, DfES.

Gibson, S., Oberg, D. and Pelz, R. (1999) *Internet Use in Alberta Schools: a multi-phase study*, www.carleton.ca/amtec99/Internet-Alberta.doc.

Grover, R., Fox, C. and Lakin, J. McM. (eds) (2001) *The Handy 5: planning and assessing integrated information skills and instruction*, Lanham, MD, Scarecrow Press.

Herring, J., Tarter, A.-M. and Naylor, S. (2002) An Evaluation of the Use of the PLUS Model to Develop Pupils' Information Skills in a Secondary School, *School Libraries Worldwide*, **8** (1), 1–24.

Hyerle, D. (2000) *A Field Guide to Using Visual Tools*, Lyme, NH, Association for Supervision and Curriculum Development.

Kent Educational Authority (2003) *How will the Internet Enhance Learning?*, www.kented.org.uk/ngfl/policy/question4.html.

Kinchin, I. and Hay, D. (2000) How a Qualitative Approach to Concept Map Analysis can be Used to Aid Learning by Illustrating Patterns of Conceptual Development, *Educational Research*, **42** (1) (Spring), 43–57.

Kyriacou, C. (1998) *Essential Teaching Skills*, 2nd edn, Cheltenham, Stanley Thornes.

Leu, D. (2002) Internet Workshop: making time for literacy, *The Reading Teacher*, (February), www.readingonline.org.

Lieberman, D. (1999) *Learning: behaviour and cognition*, 3rd edn, Florence, KY, Wadsworth.

Loertscher, D. (2000) *Taxonomies of the School Library Media Program*, 2nd edn, Spring, TX, Hi Willow Research and Publishing.

Loertscher, D. and Woolls, B. (2002) *Information Literacy: a review of the research*, 2nd edn, Spring, TX, Hi Willow Research and Publishing.

Matusevich, M. (1995) *School Reform – what role can technology play in a constructivist setting?*, http://pixel.cs.vt.edu/edu/fis/techcons.html.

Northamptonshire County Council (2000) *Developing an Internet Access Policy for Your School*, www.northants-ecl.gov.uk/apps/ICT/dia/hme.asp

Sandwell Education and Lifelong Learning (2002) *Schools Internet Access Policy*, www.lea.sandwell.gov.uk/lea/docs/schools-internet.pdf.

Schunk, D. (2000) *Learning Theories: an educational perspective*, 3rd edn, Upper Saddle River, NJ, Prentice Hall.

Slowinski, J. (1999) Internet in America's Schools, *First Monday*, **4** (1), www.firstmonday.dk/issues/issue4_1/slowinski/.

Stevens Institute of Technology (2003) *Alliance + Project*, http://k12science.ati.stevens-tech.edu/alliance/admin/resadm.html.

Thomas, N. (1999) *Information Literacy and Information Skills Instruction*, Westport, CT, Libraries Unlimited.

Tileston, D. (2000) *10 Best Teaching Practices*, Thousand Oaks, CA, Corwin Press.

Tubbs, M. (1996) *The New Teacher*, London, David Fulton Publishers.

Virtual Teacher Centre (2003) *Integrating ICT into History*, http://vtc.ngfl.gov.uk/docserver.php?temid=271.

2

The internet

. . . .

Having read this chapter, you will be able to:

* use a range of features of the internet such as e-mail, listservs and the world wide web
* evaluate the features and quality of a range of search engines used by teachers and school librarians
* effectively use search engines to support learning and teaching in your school
* keep up to date with changes in the services offered by search engines
* explore aspects of the deep web
* evaluate and implement examples of in-service training for effective search engine use in your school.

. . . .

Introduction

The internet is now commonly used in most countries in the world although access is restricted in many parts of the world because of economic difficulties. The internet has opened up many new and exciting possibilities for schools both within, e.g. e-mailing teacher to teacher, school librarian to teacher, teacher or school librarian to student/s, headteacher to staff and/or students, and outside the school, e.g. teachers and school librarians to external colleagues/contacts; students to students in other countries as part of projects or exchanges; parents to school staff. Both teachers and school librarians are often active members of listservs through which they can keep in contact with and discuss issues with fellow practitioners. When using the term 'the internet', however, many people are often referring to the web. The web is part of the internet but only one part – listservs, for example, form another part of the web. It is the use of the web which can be seen as presenting school management, teachers and school librarians with opportunities to invigorate the school curriculum and improve learning and teaching in the school. Although the web has been praised as a potentially endless source of curriculum-related information and ideas, recently there has been criticism of it. Trilling and Hood (2001), for example, argue that 'The Web is starting to look more like the world's largest shopping mall rather than a global library or communications medium', because of the increase in advertising on websites, including on those of potential use to school students. Search engines have developed as tools in recent years, but are still relatively unsophisticated: while a user of a search engine can input complex searches, there is still little interaction. Search engines are not yet capable of meaningfully questioning the user in relation to their enquiry. Therefore, search engines have yet to develop into truly intelligent agents capable of questioning and advising the user, e.g. how to restructure a search in order to find more relevant information or ideas. Developments such as the deep web or invisible web may be starting points for more meaningful information retrieval on the web.

Thus, the challenge for teachers and school librarians is how to make the best use of the various features of the internet in order to improve students' education, their own contribution to that education, and their own learning and professional development. This chapter will provide guidance in these areas by examining e-mail and listservs; search engine features and quality; effective search strategies when using search engines; keeping up to date with search engine developments; the deep or invisible web; and in-service training in relation to search engine use in schools.

E-mail and listservs

While the use of e-mail is widespread in higher education, in most UK schools and in many schools in the USA, Canada and Australia, e-mail use is restricted because of two factors. The first is that not all teachers in all schools have their own desktop and the second is that even where teachers all have their own desktop, the culture of the school has not moved on to a stage where all teachers are *expected* to check their e-mail at least once a day. For school librarians, who *do* have a desktop and who *do* check their e-mail more that once a day, this can be frustrating. At recent in-service sessions run by this author, school librarians have expressed concern that the teachers' lack of regular e-mail checking means that when the school librarian uses e-mail to send materials or information to teachers, they cannot depend on the teachers checking their e-mails, which makes it difficult to use a potentially very useful internet application in schools. Ictadvice (2003) states that the advantages of e-mail use for teachers include: 'access to professional development forums; the opportunity to contact colleagues and share good practice; and the ability to forge links that benefit the school'.

The Teachers Online Project (2003) provides a number of examples of teachers using e-mail for a variety of different applications including helping new students to settle in by encouraging them to maintain contact with a former school and e-mailing the headteacher with schemes of work from home.

E-mail projects

E-mail can also be used successfully in projects involving two or more schools. In Australia, the Netdays (2000) project involved teachers and students from a range of schools participating in a project which helped students to learn about different cultures, and students were encouraged to compare data collected via e-mail and to establish regular e-mail contact with similar students in another school. Those schools who were successful in using this kind of project to improve student learning benefited from incorporating the use of e-mail (and interactive project websites) into student learning but it was observed that e-mail projects require careful planning on the part of teachers so that they are relevant to the school curriculum and not mere add-ons. In the USA, Lerman (1998) argues that the concept of keypals, where students make contact by e-mail with students from other schools, can be a stimulating educational experience if managed well by teachers. Lerman gives an example of how to initiate an e-mail project:

Task
Write a travel brochure. Collect travel brochures from places outside your local area. Ask students to study how the brochures are put together and develop assessments of what distinguishes a good or useful brochure from one that isn't. Then, contact a class in another geographic area to be keypals with your class for this project. Develop with the keypal class an agreed-upon format for producing a travel brochure.

Lerman provides a note of caution, advising teachers to train their students well in the safe use of e-mail, not meeting e-mail contacts without teacher supervision and not sending individual photographs. Keypal sites such as ePALS Classroom Exchange (www.epals.com) and Classroom Connect Teacher Contact Database (www.classroom.net/teachercontact/) are recommended by Lerman.

Listservs

The use of listservs or discussion groups can ensure regular contact with fellow professionals and there is a number of very successful listservs for teachers and school librarians in different countries. For teachers in the UK, UK Teachers Chatboard is available at http://uk.teachers.net/chatboard/features.html. Australian teachers can join the OZ-Teachers listerv located at oz-teachers@rite.ed.qut.edu.au. In North America, US teachers can use the *Mailrings* feature at www.teachers.net/mailrings/ while Canadian teachers can use a similar feature at http://canadian.teachers.net/. For school librarians in the UK, listservs exist on both the Virtual Teacher Centre (http://vtc.ngfl.gov.uk) and the Scottish Virtual Teacher Centre (www.svtc.org.uk) but the main listserv for UK school librarians is the lively SLN (http://groups.yahoo.com/group/sln/). In Australia, the OZTL_NET listserv (www.csu.edu.au/research/cstl/oztl_net/) is very successful and is a useful resource for school librarians around the world. Even if school librarians in other countries do not regularly receive OZTL_NET e-mails which inform them of the daily topics under discussion, the archives are a very good source of information and advice about a range of current issues and about curriculum-relevant print and electronic resources. A recent example of a query sent to OZTL_NET and a reply can be seen in Figure 2.1

In North America, the LM_NET listserv (see www.askeric.org/lm_net/sub.html on how to join) is also very well used by school librarians (or library media specialists, as they are more commonly known in the USA) and, as with OZTL_NET, if school librarians do not wish to receive regular e-mails, they can check out the archives. A recent example of a query and reply can be seen in Figure 2.2.

Thus, the use of e-mail by teachers and school librarians can take many forms and can lead to extending professional contact and the sharing of ideas as well as initiating student projects. Constructive use of e-mail can be a boon to both teachers and school librarians but both should be aware of the potential

From: Elizabeth Derouet [mailto:ederouet@hotmail.com]
Sent: Thursday, 15 May 2003 02:36
To: oztl_net@listserv.csu.edu.au
Subject: [OZTL_NET] Inventions websites [Scanned]
Hello everyone
Does anyone know of any good websites suitable for grade 4 (Qld) for a unit on inventions? I will post a hit to the listserv in about a week's time with the results!

[Reply]

Elizabeth, Try these
1. Australian Inventions
http://library.trinity.wa.edu.au/subjects/te/austinv.htm
2. Inventions
http://library.trinity.wa.edu.au/subjects/te/inventions.htm
3. Medical Invention
http://library.trinity.wa.edu.au/subjects/science/medical.htm
4. Scientists and Scientific Invention
http://library.trinity.wa.edu.au/subjects/science/scientific.htm

Figure 2.1   Example from OZTL_NET listserv
(www.csu.edu.au/research/cstl/oztl_net/)

From: School Library Media & Network Communications
[mailto:LM_NET@LISTSERV.SYR.EDU]On Behalf Of Roberta Kobbe
Sent: Tuesday, April 01, 2003 9:40 AM
To: LM_NET@LISTSERV.SYR.EDU
Subject: OT: magnesium in food
These are health questions for any health gurus out there:
Calcium builds strong bones and teeth, vitamin C builds immunity and prevents scurvy, iron builds blood, etc.
What does magnesium do?
Also, what FOODS contain high amounts of magnesium? Do any?
Thanks,
Roberta Kobbe
Derby, KS
rkobbe@derby.k12.ks.us

[reply]

The National Institute of Health:
www.cc.nih.gov/ccc/supplements/magn.html#def
This is a great site - explains magnesium really well-
Basically, it helps diabetics and those with some heart problems. However, most healthy adults get all they need in the foods they eat. This page also includes a list of foods that contain magnesium.

Figure 2.2   Example from LM_NET listserv (www.askeric.org/lm_net/sub.html)

for information overload if much of the e-mail they receive is not relevant to their work in their school.

Search engines

Search engines are used daily by teachers, school librarians and students and are now recognized as the key tool to use when searching for information on the web. However, whether search engines are used *effectively* by both professionals and students is open to question. This section will seek to provide teachers and school librarians with a brief guide to exploiting the full range of search engine features in order to improve the results gained from using search engines.

Search engine definitions

Notess (1999) states that search engines are:

> huge databases of web page files that have been assembled automatically by machine. ... The term more properly refers to any software used to search any database. On the internet the phrase usually refers to the large databases of Web sites that are automatically generated.

School Libraries on the Web (2003) define search engines as tools that

> index web sites using electronic means such as spiders, robots or worms which roam the web and compile a database of information. In its basic form, the results list from a search of this database contains a list of web sites which contain that search term, and the placement of the web sites on that list is based upon the frequency of the appearance of that term, its location on the page and similar factors.

The above definitions relate to what are termed *single search engines*, among the most commonly used of which are Google, Altavista and Yahoo! School librarians and teachers can also use *metasearch engines*, which take the user's search terms and apply them to a number of single search engines. The most popular metasearch engine amongst school librarians around the world is probably Dogpile. Bradley (2002) sorts search engines into four categories, i.e.:

- free-text search engines such as AltaVista
- index- or directory-based search engines such as Yahoo!
- multi- or meta-search engines such as Dogpile
- natural-language search engines such as AskJeeves.

What is important for schools is that school managers, teachers, school librarians and students know what search engines are, what they can offer and also their limitations. The key responsibility for educating potential users of search engines in schools lies with school librarians, who are the schools' information professionals. Therefore, before educating others, school librarians should gain in-depth knowledge of search engines and their potential value in schools. Bradley's (2002) book *The Advanced Internet Searcher's Handbook* is an excellent source.

Search engine features

There are several significant features to be considered when examining search engines: school librarians, in particular, need to be aware of these so that they can advise web users in the school as to the benefits or otherwise of using particular search engines for particular purposes. It is clear that no single search engine should be used for all types of search; however, even for information professionals such as school librarians, it is easy to fall into the trap of depending completely on one search engine all the time. This is inadvisable because different search engines have different features, which can make them a more appropriate information retrieval tool for certain types of search.

Table 2.1 is part of a table from Search Engine Showdown, which compares a number of commonly used search engines. This is a good example of the type of information source that school librarians might use when advising other school web users. The key components of the table show how each search engine applies a range of search features, including:

- *Boolean*: Search engines use Boolean logic terms AND, OR and NOT to allow users to combine elements of a search. AND may be substituted by the plus (+) sign and NOT may be substituted by the minus (-) sign.

- *Default*: This shows to which aspect of Boolean logic the search engine defaults or which aspect it uses unless the searcher includes others. While

Table 2.1 Search engines features chart (from Search Engine Showdown at www.searchengineshowdown.com/features/)

Search Engines	Boolean	Default	Proximity	Truncation	Case	Fields	Limits	Stop	Sorting
Google	-, OR	AND	Phrase	No	No	intitle, inurl, more	Language, filetype, date, domain	Values, + searches	Relevance, site
AlltheWeb	AND, OR, ANDNOT, (), +, -, or with ()	AND	Phrase	No	No	title, URL, link, more	Language, filetype, date, domain	No if not rewritten	Relevance, site
Lycos	+, -	AND	Phrase	No	No	title, URL, link, more	Language, domain	No	Relevance
AltaVista Simple	+, -, AND, OR, ANDNOT, ()	AND, phrase	Phrase, NEAR	Yes	No	title, URL, link, more	Language, filetype	Yes	Relevance, site
AltaVista Adv.	AND, OR, ANDNOT, ()	Phrase	Phrase, NEAR, within, <, <~	Yes	Yes	title, URL, link, more	Language, filetype, date	No	Relevance, if used
HotBot (Inktomi)	AND, OR, NOT (), -	AND	Phrase	No	Yes	title, more	Language, date	Some	Relevance, site
MSN Search	AND, OR, NOT, (), -	AND	Phrase	No	Yes	title, link	Language, filetype, date	Some	Relevance

most search engines default to AND, AltaVista Advanced Search defaults to 'phrase'.

- *Proximity*: How near to each other words used in a search will be. Most users employ a *phrase search*, which may need the user to add inverted commas (" ") around the phrase.
- *Truncation*: Enables the user to search using part of a word, e.g. *acid** to find information on acids, acidity, acidic.
- *Case*: Most search engines will search successfully if the user enters the term in upper or lower case. Some search engines can search for the exact case, e.g. exTENT.
- *Fields*: This allows a user to search on a specific part of a website, e.g. on links or title.
- *Limits*: Allows the user to add a restriction to the search, e.g. search only sites in French.
- *Stop*: Stop words are common words which are not searchable, e.g. a, the, of.
- *Sorting*: Search engines usually sort by relevance but the user can specify that results are sorted by date or alphabetically by title.

While it is clear that not all school web searchers will need to know the intricacies of search engine features, it will be important that certain categories of student understand how to maximize their searches by using Boolean logic effectively. For example, a year 13 (final-year) secondary/high school student in England searching for information for an advanced project on the fat content of particular types of food can be advised to use a mixture of Boolean operators to enhance the quality of the search. Thus the student might enter:

fat+content+foods

which would retrieve a vast number of results. However, as the student is not examining meat-based foods as part of the study, if they entered:

fat+content+foods-meat

then the results would be more relevant.

Most search engines display their results in a list which the user can scroll down. Newer search engines such as Kartoo (www.kartoo.com) display their results as a concept map. This feature can be very useful for school students who

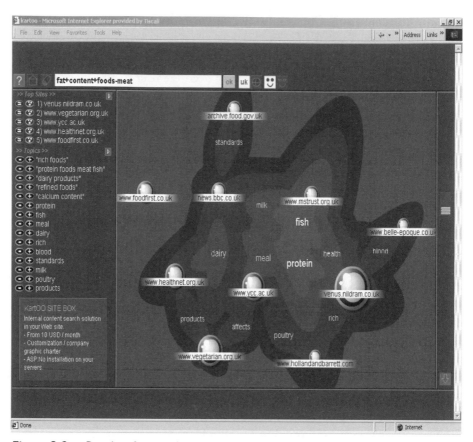

Figure 2.3   Results of a search using Kartoo (www.kartoo.com)

will use concept maps to plan their searches (see Chapter 6 for examples) and the results of a Kartoo search *may* help students to revise their concept maps. Teachers and school librarians, however, have to teach students to evaluate the results of searches, since a poor search strategy will *not* lead to Kartoo producing a relevant concept map. Figure 2.3 shows the results of the above search on Kartoo.

Search engine quality

It is a common fallacy amongst web users that there is one search engine which leads the table in terms of 'quality'. Quality may be defined in terms of *speed* – how quickly the search engine finds and presents its results; *presentation* – what information the search engine provides on each website it retrieves; or *coverage* – how widely it searches to find relevant websites. However, a search engine's quality can be evaluated only in terms of how successfully it meets the needs of an individual searcher. For example, does the search engine find websites that are *very* relevant to the search as opposed to *quite* relevant? Or does the search engine find sites that match the language level of the searcher – an important factor when school students are searching? The answer to these questions often lies not with the search engines but with the ability of searchers to define their search terms exactly and to know which search engines are most useful for different types of enquiry.

Teachers and school librarians would benefit from studying the guidance for schools provided by Noodletools (2003), which provides an excellent evaluation of search engines to suit the needs of particular users. Figure 2.4 shows how different search engines might be used for different search needs.

Teachers and school librarians need to make a clear distinction between the *most popular* search engine (usually cited as Google) and the *most appropriate* search engine as this will vary according to the need of the school web searcher. By referring to Figure 2.4, a teacher or school librarian seeking information on **global warming** might use the following search engines according to their exact need:

- *Global warming* (I want to know what's generally available on this topic) – Google
- *Global warming* (I want to update my academic knowledge on this topic) – Librarians' Index to the Internet or Pinakes
- *Global warming* (I want some popular science examples for my year 7 (11-year-old) students) – Yahoo!

Effective search strategies

An effective search strategy is one that is based on the purpose and the need of the searcher. Thus a teacher planning a lesson on the causes of earthquakes for a year 7 (first year of secondary/high school) class may have *two* purposes, i.e.:

- to find information on the causes of earthquakes in order to update the teacher's own knowledge of the topic
- to find websites that will be suitable for use by 11 to 12-year-old students with different reading levels.

Information Literacy: Search Strategies	
Choose the Best Search for Your Information Need	
Information need	Search strategy
I need a **few good hits fast**.	Google - largest index[1] results ranked by general popularity with "blind spots."[2] Caches copy of page if site unavailable. AlltheWeb - large, automatically adds phrases from its dictionary to improve relevance of results.
I have a **broad academic subject** and need pointers to quality sites.	Librarians' Index to the Internet - "thinking person's Yahoo"[3] with weekly updates. Infomine - librarian-selected directory with flexible search options.
I have a **popular or commercial topic**.	Yahoo! - user-submitted, editor-categorized commercial "tree" entries are integrated with Google search results
I want to search on **confusable** (e.g. bush v. Bush) or **ignored words** (e.g. there v. There - a company) in a **phrase** (e.g., "Vitamin A" or "to be or not to be").	AltaVista Advanced - use capital letter Google - use quotes around phrase, or +word
I can't **spell** something (e.g. "Ku Klux Klan" or "Klu Klux Klan").	Use a dictionary for the correct spelling. If an alternative spelling will generate better results Google asks you, "Did you mean: (more common spelling)?"
I need a template to **focus my search**.	AlltheWeb Advanced or AltaVista Advanced (full Boolean) template prompts you to include or exclude words and phrases, domain, format, date, etc.
I need to **organize and refine my results**.	Combined major engine results (metasearch) clustered by topics. Select keywords to pinpoint your search further. • Vivisimo - automatic clustering, hierarchical folders • SurfWax - identify promising results using preview summary ("SiteSnap"); see context of key words on the page ("ContextZooming"), add "Focus Words" to narrow next search. • Ez2Find - gathers results from top engines (results include some invisible web information) • Dogpile - "fetch" and clustered results (Vivisimo) attracts younger students. • AltaVista - displays the most common words from your results which you can add to your query for more focused results.
I need to **see relationships** among ideas.	• KartOO - intuitive interface visually "maps" relationships and refines ideas • Web Brain - visual view of related subjects. Click on term to search dmoz database, a directory compiled by volunteer editors

Figure 2.4   Advice on using different search engines from Noodletools (www.noodletools.com/debbie/literacies/information/5locate/adviceengine.html)

As will be seen in Chapters 5 and 6, teaching information skills to students who will be using the web as one source of information and ideas will focus on *identifying purpose* as one of the key skills but it is important for school librarians and teachers themselves to focus clearly on their own purpose before undertaking a search. Robert Gordon University and Queen Margaret University College (2001) advise:

> Before starting an online search ask yourself the following:
> - What is the question, what do you want information on?
> - Can you think of any related concepts?
> - For what purpose is the information required – an overview or in-depth?
> - How will the information be used, who is the audience?
> - How much information is required and when?
> - In what form is the information required?
> - How might you limit your search e.g. by year, language?
> - If English language, are there any American synonyms?
> - What resources are the most appropriate to access?
> - Do the answers to these questions indicate that online resources are best?

No matter how effectively the teacher or school librarian uses the various Boolean operators such as AND, OR, NOT, NEAR and ADJ(ACENT) in their search, if the purpose of the search is not clear, the results of the search are unlikely to be relevant.

The second key element in effective search strategies is identifying keywords which will produce relevant results. As will be seen in Chapters 5 and 6, students can be encouraged to use brainstorming and concept mapping to identify keywords from purpose but it is very important that teachers and school librarians recognize that their own searching should adopt similar rules to those which they will subsequently teach to students. Returning to the example of a teacher planning a lesson for a group of first year of secondary/high school students (year 7) on the causes of earthquakes, the teacher can consult with the school librarian on how best to go about doing an effective search on this topic. The school librarian may advise the teacher to use a subject gateway (see Chapter 4) but if one or more search engines is to be used, the teacher and school librarian can co-operate by planning a search together, combining the teacher's knowledge of the topic and the school librarian's knowledge of searching techniques. The most effective way to define a productive search strategy is to break down a statement or question into a number of related concepts. RGU/QMUC (2001) advise that the searcher writes a statement of what is needed. In this case it might be 'Information on the causes of volcanoes written in language understandable by 11 year-olds of average ability and containing graphical as well as textual information'. From this statement, RGU/QMUC advise that the searcher identifies the concepts in the statement and this might be seen as:

Concept 1	Concept 2	Concept 3	Concept 4	Concept 5
What	What 2	Where	How / Special features	When
Volcanoes	Causes	Anywhere	Level of language	Most recent

Consideration needs to be given to alternatives, e.g. the searchers in this case might want to identify the first concept as **Volcano** or **Volcanic** as well as **Volcanoes** and the school librarian might advise the use of truncation in this search, i.e. search for Volcan* as opposed to one of the other words. It is important that the level of language is considered, because much of the material on the web relating to volcanoes is academic research, useful to vulcanologists and their students in universities, but not to 11 year olds. Thinking about the concept When is also important, as this should limit the search and eliminate much of the historical evidence on volcanoes, which is not what the teacher wants. The teacher in this case may leave the agreed search with the school librarian who can e-mail the results to the teacher. The search strategy may therefore be:

Volcan* causes recent "high school"

This search includes the use of the asterisk to denote truncation and the use of inverted commas so that the search engine will look for this phrase when searching. If this search were conducted in Google, the results would be as in Figure 2.5.

If this search were conducted using Dogpile, the hits from the Teoma search engine would be as in Figure 2.6, but only if the term **volcan*** is replaced with **volcano**, as Dogpile does not make effective use of the truncation in this search..

There is no such thing as a perfect search strategy and the school librarian will have to evaluate the results of these searches to decide whether the search was effective or not. For example, if too few results emerge, the search may have to be widened using these search engines or the school librarian may

Figure 2.5 Results of a search on Google (www.google.com)

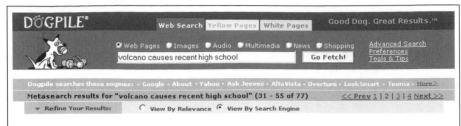

Search Engine Teoma: 10 results for "volcano causes recent high school"

1. **Biblical Plagues and Parting of Red Sea caused by Volcano**
   ... thirty miles high to be seen in Egypt. The recent Pinatubo volcano was 26 miles high. ... A volcano causes walls of ... I read that old high ...
   http://www.freerepublic.com/focus/news/786902/posts

2. **Miscellaneous Questions**
   ...information about the recent ... is a volcano and what causes ... have a list of volcano activity resources appropriate for senior high school ...
   http://volcano.und.nodak.edu/vwdocs/frequent_questions/group ...

3. **Questions about the effects of volcanoes?**
   I am a high school student at Sacred Heart in Grand Coteau ... What are the causes/effects of a volcano? ... Is all the recent cold weather caused by ...
   http://volcano.und.nodak.edu/vwdocs/frequent_questions/group ...

4. **Miscellaneous Questions**
   ...information about the recent ... is a volcano and what causes ... have a list of volcano activity resources appropriate for senior high school ...
   http://www.volcanoworld.org/vwdocs/frequent_questions/group1 ...

5. **Jacksonville High School**
   ... the path of a killer volcano. ... are two of the recent hurricanes that caused much ... Jacksonville High School Videos 1 ... deal with the causes,
   http://www.jack.sprnet.org/HS%20Lib/JHSLibrary/avlist.htm

Figure 2.6 Results of a search on Dogpile (www.dogpile.com)

decide to use a natural-language search engine such as AskJeeves, doing a search on:

Where can I find information on the causes of volcanoes suitable for high school students?

The results of this search can be seen in Figure 2.7.

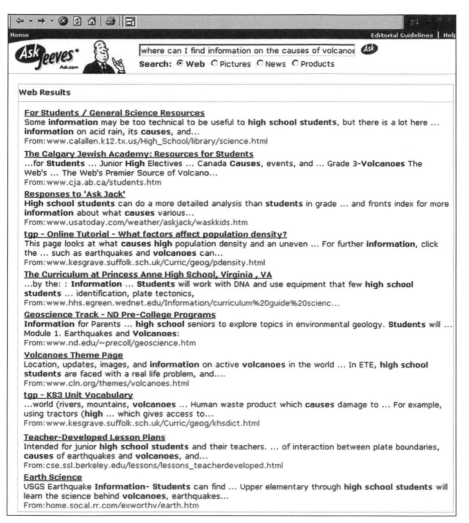

Figure 2.7   Results of a search on AskJeeves (www.ask.com)

If the results of the searches above are compared, then it can be seen that most of the sites retrieved by the search engines appear to be relevant but it is clear that AskJeeves has produced sites that seem the *most* relevant. It may be that if the word **suitable** were to be included in the other searches, then more relevant sites would have been retrieved. It is also clear from this example that by using different search engines, teachers and school librarians can improve the quality of the results gained from searching.

It can be seen that developing effective search strategies depends on a number of factors including purpose, keywords and evaluation. Experience should be added to this list as there is no doubt that the more a teacher or school librarian uses search engines, the more proficient they will become in selecting both the right keywords as well as the right search engine for a particular topic. Given that school librarians, as information professionals, are experts in information retrieval, it would be wise for teachers to consult their school librarian regularly when searches are needed. Thus a *Checklist for effective searching* for teachers to use in a school would include:

- Identify the purpose of your search – what *exactly* are you looking for?
- Who is the information for – you or your students? If students, at what stage? How important is it that the language level is suitable to students at a particular stage?
- What keywords or concepts can you identify to make your search more specific?
- Should you use Boolean logic (AND, OR, NOT) or other tools (e.g. truncation) to make your search more effective?
- Should you use the Advanced Search option in your chosen search engine?
- Once you have done your search, you need to evaluate the quality of your results and, if necessary, do the search again using more specific or more general keywords.
- You should try another search engine if your search is not successful.
- *Remember* that your school librarian is very familiar with search engines and is available to give you help and advice.

Keeping up to date with search engines

Search engines are constantly developing and gaining new features. This can be seen in the way that search engines have recently offered more services in relation to news sources, e.g. Google users can now use Google News at http://news.google.com/. Keeping up to date with search engines is useful for teachers but should be a requirement for all school librarians, who should act as the conduit for new information about search engines, which can be passed on to teachers and students. Fortunately for all librarians involved in using the web, the availability of sites such as *Search Engine Watch* (www. searchenginewatch.com) makes keeping up to date simple. This site has a number of features which are very useful to school librarians, including aspects such as advice on how to increase rankings in search engines (could be useful for the school website); how to do better searches (useful for in-service training); listings of search engines (gives details on which search engines are more suitable for use by students); search engine ratings (this reminds school librarians about the need to use different search engines); a newsletter (school librarians can check this regularly and pass on selected information/advice to teachers and/or students in the school).

Another key resource that can be used effectively in schools is *Search Engine Showdown* (www.notess.com). This site contains a range of practical and informative articles relating to all aspects of search engine use. The *Internet Resources Newsletter* (www.hw.ac.uk/libWWW/irn/irn.html) is a journal that covers a wide range of current topics relating to the web.

Keeping up to date with web developments is an important task for school librarians but it can seem overwhelming, given the number of sites which give advice on this topic. School librarians will profit from reviewing a number of sites and choosing what they see as the most useful and, where appropriate, subscribing to the site to be sent regular newsletter. It is also beneficial to do a review of web advice sites every six months, if only to gain knowledge of new sites.

The deep web

Pedley (2001) states that:

> In a white paper published by BrightPlanet, the 'invisible' or 'deep web' was said to be over 500 times larger than the 'surface web' or that part of the web to which the search engines already provide access.

Pedley notes that while some information professionals argue that the deep web is so specialized that it can be ignored, the quality of information available in the deep web is normally far higher than in sites on the 'surface web'. This is because much of the material in the deep web is in the form of databases (e.g. medical, government, scientific and legal) and the databases are organized and maintained by recognized subject experts in a wide range of fields. The best known website for the invisible web is *Complete Planet* (www.completeplanet.com), which organizes its deep web sites by categories. Other deep web specialized sites cited by Pedley of potential use to school librarians include:

- *Clip Art and Image Search* (providing sources relating to clip art but also multimedia, paintings and photographs (http://websearch.about.com/internet/websearch/msubmenu10.htm)
- *Fast Facts* (providing short factual answers to questions which might normally be answered by using reference works or fact books) (http://gwu.edu/~gprice/handbook.htm).

The deep web should not be ignored by school librarians and teachers as being too academic or too specialized as there is much information here which could be used either by teachers to increase their own subject knowledge or by final-year students who are conducting specialist assignments.

In-service training and search engines

While it may be assumed that school librarians in different countries will be familiar with the use of search engines, it is not the case that they are familiar with the range of search engines available or of the features of different search engines. In addition, surveys of teachers in countries such the UK and USA have shown that school teachers generally have little knowledge of search engines apart from very basic keyword searching. The need for in-service training both for school librarians and teachers is therefore clear and there have been many initiatives across the world to fill this need. One example is in the UK where the New Opportunities Fund (NOF), which is a lottery-related organization, has provided funding for in-service training for all teachers and school librarians in the UK from 2001. This author has been part of one of the consortia approved by NOF to run training sessions for school librarians and teachers. The Scotia Consortium (www.scotia.org.uk) organized training workshops and produced training materials according to the guidelines produced by NOF for teachers and school librarians (see www.nof.org.uk/index.cfm?loc= edu&inc=ict). The key aspects of in-service training of this type are that the training should be:

- based on training needs analysis data which is gained from teachers and school librarians completing pre-training questionnaires
- tailored to the needs of each local education authority/district: this can be achieved by both the education authority/district and the training provider analysing training needs analysis data; the result of this analysis should be

Comparing search engines

Keywords used:
Search techniques:

	Google	Yahoo!	AlltheWeb
Search options			
Number of results			
Relevance			
Annotations			
Ease of use			
Notes			

Figure 2.8   Example of in-service training workshop (copyright Robert Gordon
University and Queen Margaret University College, Scotland, UK)

the identification of any tailoring of material for local purpose.
- designed by experts in both teacher education and school librarianship, because of the overlap in the content of the training
- accompanied by workshop materials and materials to be used by trainees after the workshop sessions
- evaluated both internally, by the training providers, and externally, by independent evaluators.

An example of part of a training session relating to search engines organized and delivered by the Scotia Consortium can be seen in Figure 2.8. In this session, teachers and school librarians were asked to compare features of search engines, including search options, and then to compare the results of a search for information and images of Frank Lloyd Wright's Falling Water.

Within each school, some attention to the effective use of the web should be a part of in-service training. Given that school librarians should have an overview of the training needs of teachers in their school, they can be instrumental in convincing senior management to include web use as an in-service topic or they can design and deliver in-service sessions to teachers in the school.

Conclusion

While there are many aspects of the use of the internet in today's schools, there is no doubt that effective use of the web by teachers, school librarians and students is the most important as it is a crucial element in the delivery of the modern curriculum in schools. This chapter has sought to highlight key features of web use and suggest key sources of information which might be used by teachers and school librarians. The web is dynamic and ever changing and the one certainty is that *more* information is going to be available to schools in the future. *More* information does not mean *better* information, and the need for better search techniques and improved search engines is clear. What is also needed is clear and unambiguous guidance for teachers, school librarians and students in evaluating web resources: this is dealt with in the next chapter.

References

Bradley, P. (2002) *The Advanced Internet Searcher's Handbook*, 2nd edn, London, Library Association Publishing [3rd edn, Facet Publishing, 2004].

Ictadvice (2003) *What are the Management Issues of Teacher Access to the Web and E-Mail?*, www.ictadvice.org.uk.

Lerman, J. (1998) You've Got Mail! *Electronic School Online*, www.electronic-school.com/0398f5.html.

Netdays Australia (2000) *Cultural Journey into Australia*, http://netdays.edna.edu.au/2000.

Noodletools (2003) *Choose the Best Search for Your Information Need*,

www.noodletools.com/debbie/literacies/information/5locate/
adviceengine.html.

Notess, G. (1999) *Definitions for Terminology Used*,
www.searchengineshowdown.com/glossary.html.

Pedley, P. (2001) *The Invisible Web*, London, Aslib-IMI.

Robert Gordon University and Queen Margaret University College
(RGU/QMUC) (2001) *Library Support for ICT in the Curriculum: reader*,
RGU/QMUC (available for purchase, contact cwhitehead@rgu.ac.uk).

School Libraries on the Web (2003) *Search Engines*,
www.sldirectory.com/searchf/engines.html#engines.

Teachers Online Project (2003) *Case Studies*, http://top.ngfl.gov.uk.

Trilling, B. and Hood, P. (2001) Learning, Technology and Education Reform.
In Paechter, C. et al., *Learning, Space and Identity*, London, Paul Chapman
Publishing.

3

Evaluating websites

Having read this chapter, you will be able to:

- identify and use a range of technical criteria to evaluate websites
- identify and use a range of reliability criteria to evaluate websites
- identify and use a range of educational criteria to evaluate websites
- develop website evaluation in-service training sessions for school staff.

Introduction

As the use of the web as an information resource in schools by teachers, school librarians and students grows, it is important that all web users have the skills to evaluate the websites which they locate either by using search engines or subject gateways. While the evaluation of information has always been part of the school curriculum, e.g. in relation to either the selection of printed texts or the evaluation of information and ideas presented by authors, the difference in the *quantity* of potentially useful information resources available via the web means that there is no longer close control by teachers and school librarians over what information sources students can access. In the pre-internet past, most of the print and electronic (CD-ROM) information sources used by students were mediated by teachers and school librarians but the availability of web resources means that students are encouraged to find new information resources by themselves; these sources are *not* mediated by a teacher or school librarian if a student uses a search engine. Therefore, to compensate for this lack of control over information resources, teachers and school librarians need to educate their students on how to evaluate the websites they find. Before they can do this, teachers and school librarians need to educate themselves about the criteria that they might use to evaluate websites. For teachers, this means evaluating sites which they use to support their teaching or sites which they recommend to students via reading lists. For school librarians, this means evaluating sites which they recommend to teachers to support teaching, and those recommended to both teachers and students to support learning. This chapter will focus on the principal technical criteria which school librarians will use to evaluate websites; the reliability criteria which teachers and school librarians will use to evaluate websites; the educational criteria which teachers and school librarians will use to evaluate websites; and the potential content of in-service training sessions on website evaluation.

Technical criteria

There are many websites covering evaluation criteria; teachers and school librarians may wish to review a number of such sites. Much detailed attention is paid to the technical aspects of websites; this author would include, among technical criteria, elements of design as well as criteria relating to speed, to browsers and to special software. A number of universities have provided advice that can also be applied to websites used in schools. For example, the College of New Caledonia Library (2003) states that evaluation of technical criteria should include questions such as:

- Does the page load quickly?
- Are there any 'dead links' (connections to other pages or sites that don't work properly)?
- Did you need to upgrade your browser or install any special software or 'plug-ins' to view any of the content? If so, what was needed? Was it easy to install? Was it free or pay-for-use? Are these special technical requirements suitable to the audience the site wishes to attract?
- Does the site work with various browsers (Netscape, Internet Explorer, Opera etc.)?
- Does the page look good/still work on various screen sizes?

ED's Oasis (2003) provides a useful and useable table for school librarians and teachers to score websites according to a range of criteria. Figure 3.1 suggests criteria to evaluate the technical aspects of websites.

Element	Needs Improvement	Shows Promise	Strength Area
Connections	This site dead-ends. There aren't any links to other online resources. (0 points)	The site contains links to other resources, but they are not described. (1 point)	This site links out to other well-described resources on the same topic. (2 points)
Design	This site just isn't put together well! The colors are distracting, the words are hard to read. The layout makes it hard to use the site. (0 points)	The site is well designed and generally appealing. (1 point)	The site is visually appealing and uses colors and graphics to enhance the impact of the information. (2 points)
Navigation	Getting around is confusing. It's easy to feel lost. (0 points)	You can find your way around, but sometimes feel like you have to click too many times to get to the section you want. (1 point)	Getting from one section to another on the site is made easier by the use of pull-down menus, an index, a site map, table of contents, or other easy-to-use navigational tool. (2 points)
Technical features	Web technology is NOT used effectively. High-tech features on the site distract from the site's purpose, or make it slow or likely to crash. (0 points)	Web technology is generally used effectively. However, if the site features "new" tech goodies, like shockwave, sound, Java and animation, they seem to be unrelated to the instructional purpose. (1 point)	Web technology is used effectively. If the site features "new" tech goodies, like shockwave, sound, Java and animation, they are used to make the information more clear. (2 points)

Figure 3.1 ED's Oasis guide to website evaluation: technical criteria
(www.classroom.com/edsoasis)

Hains (2002) states that, in relation to technical aspects of websites, the following should be addressed:

- Format content effectively and break the content into screen-sized sections
- Use navigational transitions (e.g., links, headings, bullet points, hot areas, graphics) versus transitional rhetoric? (e.g., terms such as "consequently," "subsequently," "it follows that," which are based on information that either precedes or following them)
- Use graphics and features that contribute to *conveying* its message, rather than *detracting* or *distracting* from its message.

Schrock (1999) is one of the leading writers on evaluating websites in schools and, in relation to technical aspects, advises that teachers and school librarians pay particular attention to:

Efficiency If you plan to use a site with a large group of students, it is important to try it at all times of day. Some sites get very busy at midday and may slow down your lesson. If there are large graphics on the page, make sure the page resides in your cache to speed up the download time.

Schrock also argues that attention should be paid to graphics in relation to the following:

- bandwidth available in the school
- accessibility by all users, including those with a visual disability who will need a facility which allows them to view the site using text only
- the design of the site (if the site is poorly designed and contains grammar or spelling errors it is unlikely to be reliable)
- navigation – a site should be easy to use: it should contain a search function and students should immediately be aware of how the site is organized and how they can move from one part to another.

When evaluating a website from a technical point of view, the following key questions are very important:

- Can the site be used not only by Internet Explorer but by other browsers?
- Can the site be used immediately and without interruption or are there constant requests to 'plug in' software?
- Do the links work?
- Can you move around the site effectively, e.g. is there a link to the home

page on all other pages?
- Do the graphics on the site distract from its purpose, slowing down access?
- Can the site easily be used by someone with a visual handicap?

Reliability criteria

In relation to reliability criteria, the question that teachers and school librarians should ask is: 'Can I trust this site for my own purpose?' Examples of purpose can range from using a site to extend and update the teacher's knowledge of a curricular area to guiding students to a site which will reinforce what the teacher has taught in the classroom. The College of New Caledonia Library (2003) argues that in relation to 'credibility' website evaluators should ask whether the site gives clear indication of the author's or the organization's name. This should be accompanied by information which allows the user to judge its credibility, e.g. whether it is a government department or a protest movement. There should also be a facility for the website user to contact the author or organization, in a form which is more than an e-mail address. A site's reliability can also be judged on whether it is rated high in a search engine list or whether it is included in an educational subject gateway.

The ED's Oasis (2003) table again provides teachers and school librarians with a useful guide to reliability criteria including those shown in Figure 3.2.

Schrock's (1999) advice on website evaluation is very pertinent in relation to reliability criteria and she argues that teachers and school librarians will benefit from paying attention to aspects such as authority, i.e. is the author a recognized authority on a topic or a recognized organization? Schrock rightly highlights the potential bias of sites by providing the following advice:

> **Bias** Biased sites contain words that try to persuade rather than inform. Some of these words include over-generalizations and simplifications and may also contain games, giveaways, contests, or celebrity endorsements intended to persuade. Some things to think about include:
> • Is it clear what organization is sponsoring the page?
> • Is there a link to the sponsoring organization's Web site?
> • Is the page actually an ad disguised as information?

Other aspects which Schrock focuses on include whether there is an easily visible date on the website and when it was last updated; whether the site contains

Element	Needs Improvement	Shows Promise	Strength Area
Standards	Goals and objectives are not clear and/or there is no reference to standards. (0 points)	There is some mention on the site, in the Teacher's Guide section, or elsewhere, of goals, objectives, and their relation to standards. (3 points)	Goals and objectives are clearly stated and are matched to standards. (6 points)
Authority	You can not figure out who authored the content or whether the author is a reliable expert. (0 points)	The author or producer of the site is identified, but there is no background information available. (2 points)	You can tell who created the site, and you can learn about the person and his or her professional credentials. (4 points)
Interactivity	You can't email anyone or leave a message on a bulletin board or contribute your ideas anywhere on the site! (0 points)	It is possible to contact someone through this site, but you can tell messages aren't screened because you see irrelevant or inappropriate messages. (3 points)	You can use the site to get a message to subject-area experts, to the author of the site, or to exchange data and ideas with other students. No irrelevant or inappropriate messages appear on the site. (6 points)
Tone	There is evidence of disrespect or hate toward a person or a group. (0 points)	There is evidence of bias or unexplained negativity on the site. (1 point)	Neutral or positive attitudes pre-dominate on the site. Any bias is mitigated through background information on the perspective or context of the author and/or information. (2 points)

Figure 3.2   ED's Oasis guide to website evaluation: reliablity criteria
(www.classroom.com/edsoasis)

misinformation, i.e. it purports to be neutral and hides its bias behind clever design; and whether the site is 'verifiable', i.e. can the information be verified in another print or electronic source?

Teachers and school librarians should focus on the following questions in evaluating the reliability of sites they find:

- Can I trust this site because I recognize the author or organization as a reliable source of information?
- Am I able to contact the site's author for further information?
- Is the site rated highly by a search engine or subject gateway?
- Has the site been updated recently? (This is *not* the same as asking whether the site is up to date. Information that is ten years old may still be useful, but the site will be reliable only if the site itself has been updated and the information checked.)
- Is the site up to date? (This is important only if you need *current* information for a particular purpose, e.g. news information).
- Is the site *unreasonably* biased? (There is no such thing as a totally *un*biased site. For example, two environmental sites produced by (a) a government department, and (b) a protest group such as Greenpeace, may both be reliable although they take a different perspective (bias?) on environmental issues: they may not, however, be *unreasonably* biased. However, a racist, sexist or politically extreme site *will* be unreasonably biased.)
- Does the site contain misinformation or does it deliberately try to mislead the reader? (November (1998) provides an excellent review of how to identify misinformation.)

Educational criteria

The term 'educational criteria' might also be phrased as 'curricular criteria', or 'learning criteria' or 'content criteria', meaning the fundamental, essential criteria according to which teachers and school librarians should evaluate websites for either teaching or learning purposes. The key question here is: 'Is this site related to and useful for what is to be taught or learned in *this* part of the school curriculum?' Thus, the exact purpose for which the site will be used needs to be examined. For example, if a geography teacher has year 7 (first year secondary/high school) students studying the causes and environmental effects of earthquakes, and the school librarian is conducting a search for useful sites, their evaluation criteria will have to be related not just to the subject of earth-quakes but to the *purpose* identified by the teacher. This purpose may be broken down into a series of questions relating to the criteria to be used, e.g.:

* Does the site contain information on the causes of earthquakes?
* Does the site contain information on the environmental effects of earth-quakes?
* Is the level of language in the site suitable for the *range* of reading abilities in this year 7 class?
* Does the site contain useful graphics that can be used by year 7 students?

The teacher and school librarian will, of course, apply the same technical and reliability criteria outlined above but it is clear that not *all* the technical or con-tent criteria will apply (e.g. year 7 students may not need to search within the sites).

The ED's Oasis (2003) table is again relevant here and identifies useful cri-teria, e.g. whether the site contains activities for students and whether the site encourages students to think critically about the topic. This can be seen in Figure 3.3.

Teachers and school librarians can benefit from asking the following ques-tions when evaluating websites:

* Is the content of this site related to my purpose?
* Is the language used at the right level for my students? (Differentiation will need to be considered here as there will be a range of reading levels in one class.)
* Will the website provide students with any activities? (Some sites include educational games or quizzes which may be suitable.)
* Will the website inspire or motivate my students? (This includes whether the website is likely to pose relevant questions which encourage critical thinking amongst students.)
* Does the website contain suitable graphics which students can study or use? (This will be particularly important for science or geography sites where one of the teacher's aims is for all students to gain experience of using graphs or maps.)

Element	Needs Improvement	Shows Promise	Strength Area
Curriculum	The site is unrelated to what students typically study. (0 points)	This site is somewhat related to what students might study in a core subject or elective course. (3 points)	This site is clearly related to what students might study in a core subject or an elective course and can be used to support, enrich, or extend student learning. (6 points)
Activity helpers	The site does NOT contain suggestions for how students can conduct investigations, create presentations, or complete projects. (0 points)	The site contains suggestions for how students can conduct investigations, create presentations, or complete projects. (2 points)	The site includes graphic organizers, templates or forms to help with student work. (4 points)
Grade Level	No grade level is specified on the site, OR the specified grade level is too broad to be meaningful. (0 points)	Material on the site, or the activities it contains are NOT well-matched to its target audience. The reading level is too high or too low, or the activities are either too complex or too simple. (2 points)	Material and activities on the site are well-matched to the target audience. (4 points)
Information Quality	The material on this site is old and flat. It does not inspire students to come up with new thoughts and ideas. (0 points)	The material on this site is interesting, but does not motivate students to generate new ideas, or participate in learning activities. (3 points)	The material on this site helps students think up great ways to do projects. The site helps students think creatively and/or critically. (6 points)

Figure 3.3   ED's Oasis guide to website evaluation: educational criteria (www.classroom.com/edsoasis)

In-service training

Given that all teachers will be encouraging their students to use websites as a key source of information, it is important for teachers and school librarians to recognize the importance of in-service training in relation to this topic. There is much competition for the content of in-service training days in schools, so teachers and school librarians who want to promote the topic of evaluating websites for inclusion in in-service training will have to identify key reasons to justify this to senior management. The justification for including evaluating websites could be presented as follows:

- Teachers' use of websites is increasing and they need the skills to evaluate them.
- Teachers' ability to educate students in website evaluation will be enhanced via this in-service training.
- Student learning will be enhanced if they can be taught effective website evaluation.

Figure 3.4 is an example of an in-service training session this author designed for use with school librarians, but it could easily be used with teachers in a school as well. One of the key purposes of this session was to encourage *critical appraisal* both of websites and of the model used. The CARS model (www. sccu.edu/faculty/R_Harris/evalu8it.htm) is a useful guide to evaluating websites but it is clearly designed more for university students: for example, it puts no emphasis on the level of language in a site, which is a crucial element in website evaluation for educators in schools. Encouraging teachers in a school to develop their *own* list or model is a means of developing ownership of the topic as opposed to depending on an external model.

Conclusion

This chapter has sought to provide a guide to evaluating websites for teachers and school librarians. There is no definitive guide on this topic, but there are many models available and it would be sensible for each school to have its own set of guidelines, proposed initially by the school librarian and then discussed with teachers from different subject areas. This would provide the basis for a whole-school policy on evaluating websites which could be used by all staff in the school. This could then be adapted to provide guidelines for students at different levels in the school, ranging from simple advice for the lower end of the school and more sophisticated advice (e.g. on the political or philosophical stance of a website) for the upper end of the school. If

---

Evaluating websites
Seminar for school librarians

Aims
This seminar aims to:
* establish a set of criteria for evaluating websites
* examine critically the CARS model
* discuss ways and advantages of getting teachers and/or pupils/students to evaluate websites

Methodology
1. Each librarian should look at the following websites and make notes on each one, to indicate whether it might or might not be useful for different levels of pupil in their schools:
   (a) www.windows.ucar.edu - a website for school children on the universe.
   (b) www.sepa.org.uk - a government website on the environment
   (c) www.diabetes.org.uk - the website of the British Diabetes Association
   (d) www.geo.mtu.edu/volcanoes - volcanoes website
2. Each group will examine the CARS model and discuss its merits and limitations - **5 minutes**
3. Each group will compare their notes on the websites viewed and discuss to what extent they used the CARS criteria or other criteria - **10 minutes**
4. Each group will discuss ways and advantages of getting teachers and pupils/students to evaluate websites - **5–10 minutes**
5. Each group will draw up a list indicating what their agreed criteria might be (rank your criteria in importance and restrict your criteria to 5 points) – **5–10 minutes**
6. There will be a comparison of the groups' criteria and discussion of evaluation - **10 minutes**

Figure 3.4   In-service training session for school librarians

staff and students feel that they own their guidelines, they are more likely to use them effectively.

References

College of New Caledonia Library (2003) *Evaluating Websites – questions to ask*, www.cnc.bc.ca/library/evaluatingwebsites.html.

ED's Oasis (2003) *Web Site Evaluation for Educators*, www.classroom.com/edsoasis.

Hains, A. (2002) *Considerations for Website Users*, www.uwm.edu/~annhains/appendix_b.htm.

November, A. (1998) *Teaching Zach to Think*,
    www.anovember.com/articles/zack.html.
Schrock, K. (1999) *The ABCs of Website Evaluation*,
    http://school.discovery.com/schrockguide/pdf/weval.pdf.

4

Subject gateways

....

Having read this chapter, you will be able to:

- evaluate subject gateways as potential sources of learning and teaching materials
- identify and use a range of general curriculum-related subject gateways
- identify and use a range of subject-specific gateways
- identify and use a range of commercially available subject gateways and online sources
- develop an in-service training session in relation to subject gateways.

....

Introduction

Subject gateways are useful tools for teachers and school librarians who want to find relevant, up-to-date and previously evaluated learning and teaching information resources. Chapter 3 examined the use of search engines as tools for finding educational resources but it can be argued that subject gateways are more effective tools for teachers and school librarians because they are less general than search engines. Therefore, subject gateways can be seen having the following advantages over search engines:

- General subject gateways cover specific areas – e.g. education – while search engines cover the whole spectrum of information.
- Subject specific gateways focus on a particular topic – e.g. health sciences – while search engines include a wider context for such topics.
- Subject gateways include lists of sites which have been submitted or evalu-

ated by subject experts such as teachers or school librarians, while search engines list sites which may *not* have been evaluated except by their authors.
• Subject gateways provide access to other tools such as listservs, while search engines only provide lists of sites.

Subject gateways are valuable sources of information for teachers and school librarians; while they have advantages over search engines in some respects, as seen above, this does not mean that using a subject gateway will *always* produce more relevant, up-to-date and curriculum-related information than a search engine. The outcome will depend on what the teacher or school librarian is seeking for a particular purpose. For example, if a school librarian is advising a senior student on how to find information for a final year assignment on **diabetes**, a health subject gateway should provide relevant information, but an advanced search on Google may, in some cases, provide a better range of sources. So, subject gateways should not be seen as replacements for search engines but rather as alternative tools that may be more effective in directing the searcher to relevant and trustworthy sources.

There is a range of different types of subject gateway and this chapter will examine:

• how to evaluate subject gateways
• general subject gateways used in schools
• subject-specific gateways available to teachers and school librarians
• commercially available subject gateways and online sources
• examples of in-service training in relation to subject gateways.

Evaluating subject gateways

While subject gateways provide specific sources of information such as selected websites, lesson plans, in-service training sessions, listservs and professional groups, it is important that teachers and school librarians evaluate the gateways before using them for teaching and learning in the school. The evaluation criteria to be used should include:

• Does the subject gateway provide resources at the required level?
• Can the subject gateway resources be used without adaptation by a teacher or school librarian?

- Is there a bias in the subject gateway towards one country's national curriculum?
- Does the subject gateway list sites which contain advertising or need specific software, e.g. Shockwave or Flash?
- Is it clear from the subject gateway how sites have been submitted or evaluated by educational professionals?
- Is the subject gateway suitable for use by students as well as teachers and school librarians?

Subject gateways should guide teachers and school librarians to sources which will suit students at a particular level. Thus it should be possible to search for sites on earthquakes for year 1 secondary/high school pupils as opposed to searching for *any* sites on this topic. (See The Gateway, Blue Web'n and The Virtual Teacher Centre below.) Subject gateways will provide teachers and librarians with a vast range of resources but it is often difficult to find resources which exactly fit the need of particular students in a particular class in a school. In this case, it may be better to use a search engine, e.g. Dogpile, to find resources or to place a message on a listserv, asking colleagues if they have ideas. Or it may be that teachers and school librarians will have to accept that while the resources found on the subject gateway are useful, they may need to be adapted to suit the needs of a particular school or curriculum. For example, a lesson plan on earthquakes from Blue Web'n may contain good ideas at the right language level but teachers in Australia or the UK may have to adapt some of the terminology to suit their specific needs. One way for teachers and school librarians to contribute to the resources available is to select a website or lesson plan, adapt it for their own use and resubmit it to the gateway.

Subject gateways reflect the countries and cultures in which they were created, so teachers and school librarians must be careful when using sites found in gateways because there may be a bias towards a particular curriculum or views of a particular culture. Thus, sites on aspects such as the environment or poverty may have a cultural bias; these topics may be seen quite differently in the 'developed' countries and in 'third world' countries. Educators also need to make students aware that there may be different interpretations of the terms 'developed' and 'third world'.

One of the advantages cited about subject gateways in education is that they are much less likely to feature advertising than search engines. Although the subject gateway itself may not feature advertising, there is no guarantee that there will be no advertising on the sites found when searching. In addition, some sites listed by educational gateways will need specific software, which can limit their use. A recent discussion on the UK SLN listserv on subject gateways included a comment from school librarian Judith Sprawling:

> I found that their usefulness was limited because they didn't have a range of sites for the topic [and] had sites that needed things like Shockwave, which school networks tend not to have, to stop students playing games ...

Teachers and school librarians also need to be aware of the mechanisms for submitting sites to a subject gateway and also how sites are evaluated before being added to the gateway, e.g. are they evaluated by subject experts? A number of gateways (e.g. see Blue Web'n and Schoolzone below) rate sites by awarding them stars but it is important that teachers and school librarians understand the rating system and the criteria, e.g. for awarding a site five stars or two stars. What is crucial here is that one teacher's or school librarian's evaluation of a site as five star may not be the same as another's because of the different purposes for which the site might be used.

Finally, while it is clear that subject gateways are very useful tools for teachers and school librarians, these professionals will have to decide whether particular subject gateways are useful to their students. It is likely that subject-specific gateways may be useful to students at the upper end of secondary/high school but most gateways are not suitable for students in upper primary/elementary school or lower secondary/high schools.

General subject gateways

There is a number of subject gateways which seek to cover the full range of school subjects and which can be used by teachers and school librarians for the purposes outlined above. In the UK, both the Virtual Teacher Centre (http://vtc.ngfl.gov.uk) and the Scottish Virtual Teacher Centre (www.svtc.org.uk/) are government-funded gateways. The Virtual Teacher Centre's Teacher Resource Exchange allows the user to search by topic and by level. Figure 4.1 shows the results of a search for **earthquakes** for key stage 3 (years 7, 8 and 9 in secondary/high school).

One of the added value elements of this gateway is that searchers can view not only the materials but also comments from other users.

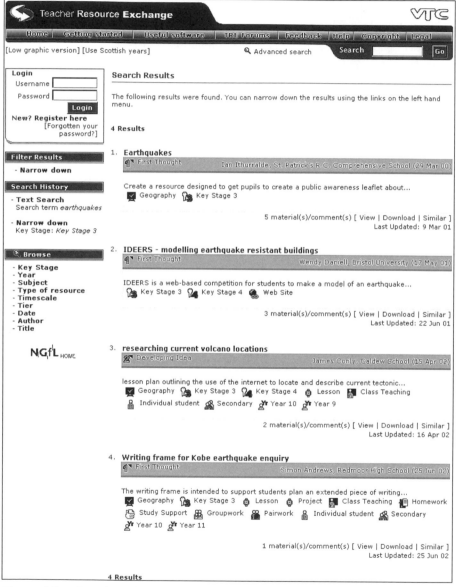

Figure 4.1   Search results from the Virtual Teacher Centre (http://vtc.ngfl.gov.uk)

search the webguide

home
teachers
students
parents
schools
business
myzone
register now
offers

Over 40,000 educational websites - all reviewed by UK teachers.
✱ rating is for educational website content. Items on a coloured background are Schoolzone pages. To search only Schoolzone's own pages use **site search**

search `earthquakes`

subject `all`

categories

age range `KS3 Ages 11 - 13`

order `rating` items/page `20`

tips on how to use   **add a link**   **go →**

other searches:
► reviews
► events
► suppliers
► schools
► tutors
► software: REM

Schoolzmail

search for:

search webguide :

go →

feedback

search results found 8 records: showing page 1 of 1

Earth Science (KS3 Ages 11 - 13) **rating** ✱ ✱ ✱ ✱ ✱
(Science, General, General) Our new educational software title, Earth Science, is an interactive multimedia CD-ROM that helps users explore our Earth system. The CD-ROM presents information on 10 areas of earth phenomena: clouds, earthquakes, forests, global warming, great lakes, the ocean, ozone, polar ice, volcanoes, and wetlands.
Translate this page

Earthquakes (KS3 Ages 11 - 13/KS4 Ages 14 - 16) **rating** ✱ ✱ ✱ ✱
(Geography, For Everyone, General) American site with many photographs explaining where and why earthquakes can occur.
Translate this page

Geography Exchange (KS3 Ages 11 - 13/KS4 Ages 14 - 16) **rating** ✱ ✱ ✱
✱
(Geography, General, General) Geography site with wealth of information for teachers and students. Includes revision, lesson ideas and web site links.
Translate this page

The San Andreas fault and the Bay Area (KS3 Ages 11 - 13/KS4 Ages 14 - 16) **rating** ✱ ✱ ✱ ✱
(Geography, Geography, Geography) Geological details and images from the San Andreas Fault zone A good guide to the most recent activity on the fault. Good images taken from aircraft
Translate this page

Earthquake Lesson Plan (KS3 Ages 11 - 13/KS4 Ages 14 - 16) **rating** ✱ ✱
✱ ✱
(Geography, General, Lessons and Worksheets) Role playing lesson plan investigating Earthquakes
Translate this page

Event-Based Science (KS3 Ages 11 - 13/KS4 Ages 14 - 16) **rating** ✱ ✱ ✱
(Science, Environment, Geography) Site designed by Public schools in Maryland to teach Science in middle schools.
Translate this page

LAYERS OF THE EARTH - lesson plan (KS3 Ages 11 - 13/KS4 Ages 14 - 16) **rating** ✱ ✱ ✱
(Geography, Geography, Environment) This is an introductory lesson that can be expanded into the following areas: Geology, volcanoes, earthquakes, and archaeology.
Translate this page

The Virtual Times Recent Earthquakes and Volcanoes (KS3 Ages 11 - 13/KS4 Ages 14 - 16) **rating** ✱ ✱
(Geography, Education resources, Environment) Site giving map with locations of volcanoes and earthquakes, clicked on gives pictures and information. Links to other sites E.g. U.S. Radar weather maps from space. Gives information in an index of volcanic and earthquake activity dated with most recent. Gives Canadian and American earthquakes in last 14 days. Suitable for keystage 3 and 4
Translate this page

Figure 4.2   Search results from Schoolzone
(www.schoolzone.co.uk)

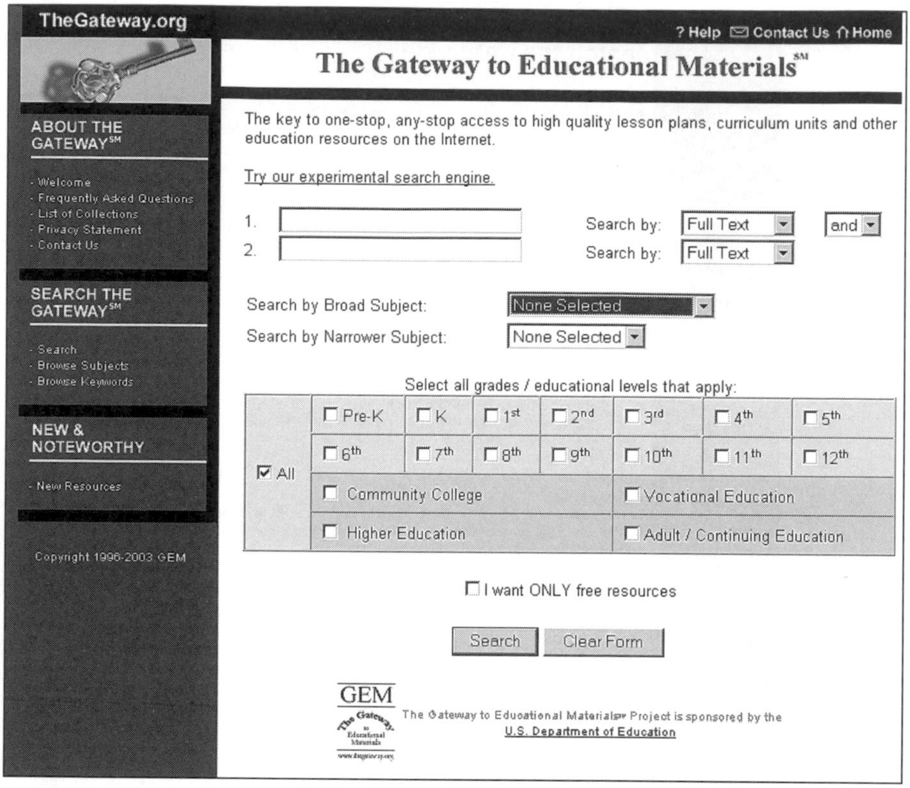

Figure 4.3   Search page for The Gateway (www.thegateway.org)

One of the best known subject gateways in the UK is Schoolzone (www.schoolzone.co.uk) which is an independent gateway organized by teachers. Using the advanced search option, a teacher or school librarian can search both by subject and by level. Figure 4.2 shows the results of the same search which was carried out on the Teacher Resource Exchange.

The results from Schoolzone demonstrate that searching on different gateways for similar materials may produce different results. Thus the Teacher Resource Exchange results are clearly materials for teachers while the Schoolzone results may be suitable for direct use by students. It should also be noted that the first site on the Schoolzone list, which is awarded five stars, is a commercial website offering a CD-ROM for sale. Teachers and school librarians therefore need to be aware that although access to most gateways and to most of the materials found is free, this is not always the case.

In North America, a commonly cited source of information for schools is

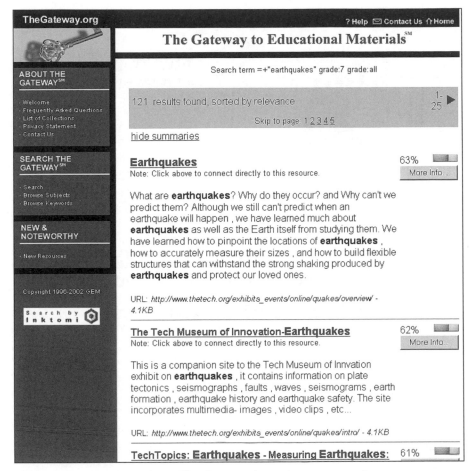

Figure 4.4   Search results on The Gateway (www.thegateway.org)

The Gateway to Educational Materials (www.thegateway.org) and as with the UK examples above, it can be searched by both subject and level. Figure 4.3 shows the search page for The Gateway and Figure 4.4 shows the results of a search for **earthquakes** for grade 7.

One of the gateways used by school librarians in many different countries is Blue Web'n (www.kn.pacbell.com/wired/bluewebn). This gateway contains a wide range of materials and information and can be searched in various ways. One particularly useful element of Blue Web'n is the table of 'Content Areas' which contains a variety of sources, from subject-related websites to lesson plans. Figure 4.5 shows the Blue Web'n home page and the options available to

Figure 4.5   Blue Web'n home page (www.kn.pacbell.com/wired/bluewebn)

HOME ABOUT THIS SITE SEARCH BROWSE WEEKLY UPDATES HOT SITE SUGGEST A LINK							
BLUE WEB'N Content Areas	References & Tools	Unit & Lesson Plans	Hotlists	Other Resources	Web Based Tutorials	Web Based Activities	Web Based Projects
Arts	19	41	35	172	10	75	5
Business	3	8	8	38	3	19	1
Community Interest	79	11	40	214	10	62	5
Education	44	32	56	295	16	47	15
English	23	43	30	203	8	118	15
Foreign Language	10	6	15	49	4	21	
Health & Physical Education	7	10	22	89	1	27	3
History & Social Studies	51	78	59	455	2	184	44
Mathematics	19	40	22	104	8	83	16
Science	48	109	43	402	22	213	63
Technology	44	12	23	168	27	27	18
Vocational Education	10	17	4	73	9	28	1

Quick Search: [enter one or two key words here]   [SEARCH]

Turn Web resources into online activities with

Filamentality

HOME ABOUT THIS SITE SEARCH BROWSE WEEKLY UPDATES HOT SITE SUGGEST A LINK

First posted 1995.
Blue Web'n content is updated weekly
© Copyright SBC Knowledge Network Explorer 1995-2003.

Figure 4.6   Materials available on Blue Web'n (www.kn.pacbell.com/wired/bluewebn)

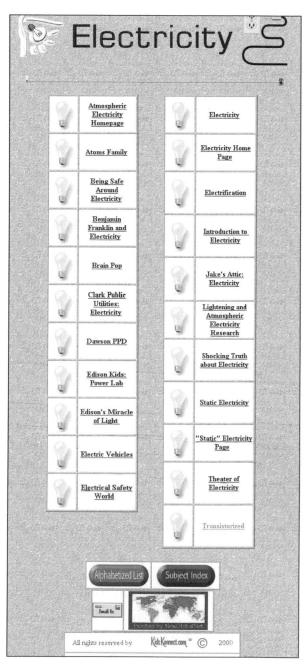

Figure 4.7   Sources on electricity from KidsKonnect
(www.kidskonnect.com)

users and Figure 4.6 shows the range of materials and information available. At the foot of Figure 4.6, there is the option to choose 'Filamentality', which allows teachers and school librarians to develop their own school-specific resources using online sources found via Blue Web'n or other gateways.

One general subject gateway designed for use by students and parents is the well known KidsKonnect (www.kidskonnect.com) site which has an alphabetized list of subjects and topics, which when clicked provides the user with a gateway to related sites. Figure 4.7 shows an example on **electricity** from KidsKonnect.

Subject-specific gateways

A wide range of subject-specific gateways can be accessed either via more general gateways or directly. However, most of the subject-specific gateways are either for use by the general public or geared mainly towards university students. This does not mean that these gateways are not useful to teachers, school librarians and students in schools but their use has to be more selective and their content may be more useful to teachers and school librarians and senior-school students.

Subject-specific gateways based in the UK are available via JISC (www. jisc.ac.uk) and via the Resource Discovery Network (RDN) (http://rdn.ac.uk) and are useful sources for teachers wishing to update their knowledge, for school librarians who are advising teachers and students and for senior secondary/high school students doing advanced level work. Figure 4.8 shows an example of GEsource, a geography subject gateway available on both the JISC and RDN sites. The site can be searched both by keyword and subject.

Commercially available subject gateways and online sources

The general and subject-specific gateways outlined above are free resources but there is a range of fee-based gateways and online sources available to schools. An excellent example of this type of gateway is WebLinks, which is a commercial service provided to schools in Australia, South Africa and the UK. Figure 4.9 shows the services offered to Australian teacher–librarians.

Much online information was once affordable only by large companies, but many schools in different countries now subscribe to online sources. For example, Ripon Grammar School in the UK used the school's e-credit funding to

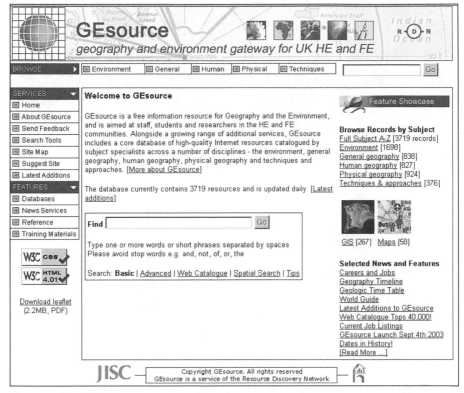

Figure 4.8 GEsource – a geography subject gateway (www.gesource.ac.uk)

buy subscriptions to Newsbank (www.newsbank.com), Britannica Online (www.britannica.com), Science Source Online (www.thesciencesource.com) and World Book Online (www.worldbookonline.com). These are available from the library across the school network via the ALICE circulation system.

In-service training

In-service training sessions for groups of teachers or school librarians (or both) can help to raise awareness of a range of subject gateways and encourage participants to discuss potential uses of gateway content. Figure 4.10 shows an example of an in-service training session developed by this author for school librarians.

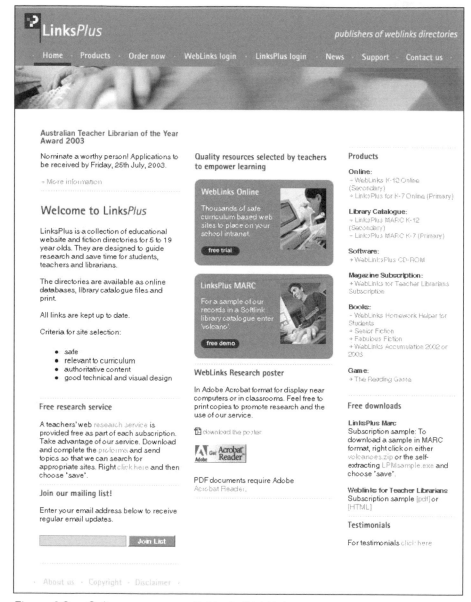

Figure 4.9   Online resources available via WebLinks
(www.weblinksresearch.com.au)

Workshop for school librarians on educational gateways

SCOTIA consortium

Exercise 1: Scottish Virtual Teacher Centre

1. Go to www.svtc.org.uk/
2. Select 3-14 and S Grade
3. Select 5-14
4. Select either **The Romans** (page 2) or **Victorian Britain** (page 1)
5. Look at the different elements on the site and write down what you would recommend about this site to a) a 2nd year student and b) a teacher looking for information on this topic
6. Go back to the home page and select Post 16 and FE
7. Select FE
8. Choose one of the subject areas from the list on the left hand side
9. Look at 3 of the sites and write down whom you might recommend these sites to in the public library and why you'd recommend them.

Exercise 2: LEARN

1. Go to www.learn.co.uk/
2. Select **Science** from the **Key Stage 3 Lessons and Tests** section (Key Stage 3 =Years 1 and 2 in a Scottish secondary school)
3. Choose one of the topics e.g. **Human Nutrition**
4. Look at some of the content on your topic and write down what you would recommend about this site to a) a 2nd year student and b) a teacher looking for information on this topic.

Exercise 3: Schoolzone

1. Go to www.schoolzone.co.uk/
2. In the **Search** box, type in **Volcanoes** and click on **GO**
3. Choose one of the websites and write down your evaluation of the site in relation to:
   - Authority - can you tell if this is a reputable site?
   - Language - who would it be suitable for in a secondary school?
   - Graphics - is there good use of graphics?
   - Links - what links are provided and are they helpful?

Exercise 4: Blue Web'n

1. Go to www.kn.pacbell.com/wired/bluewebn
2. Scroll down to the bottom of the page and do a search for **Volcanoes**
3. Write down how you think **Blue Web'n** compares to **Schoolzone**.

The group will form into sub-groups of 3/4 to discuss their findings and there will be a general discussion on issues.

Figure 4.10 Example of in-service training session on subject gateways

Conclusion

For teachers and school librarians, using subject gateways can be beneficial in that they provide professionally mediated online sources of information on virtually all aspects of the school curriculum. Gateways can also be seen, in cases such as Blue Web'n, as a 'one-stop shop' for resources which include websites for both learning and teaching as well as lesson plans and student activities. By using gateways, teachers and school librarians can save time and avoid reinventing the wheel by learning from fellow professionals as well as contributing their own ideas to the gateways, thereby extending the corporate knowledge of educators across the world.

5
Information skills

With Anne-Marie Tarter

••
Having read this chapter, you will be able to:

*   understand the nature of information literacy
*   understand the interrelated nature of skills in the PLUS model
*   critically evaluate a number of information skills models
*   learn from a range of examples how students can be taught
    information skills related to using web resources
*   apply ideas for information skills in-service training sessions.
••

Introduction

There now exists a vast literature on information skills and information literacy and teachers and school librarians seeking to improve their students' learning will benefit from examining both theoretical and practical approaches to developing information literacy in their schools. There is no doubt that students' increased use of the web in schools has increased the need for effective teaching of a range of interrelated skills which students need when using print and electronic information resources. There has been an encouraging increase in the emphasis being put on information literacy in many countries recently and it is now recognized that information literacy is important not only for learning in schools and possibly in higher education but in lifelong learning. As more and more information is being presented in society in an electronic form – e.g. the push for e-government in most countries in the world – the need for all citizens to have the relevant skills to know what they are looking for, to find and evaluate this information, to utilize this information for a purpose and to learn from the process of finding and using electronic information, should now be an urgent priority for all governments.

Skills – purpose	Questions
• Cognitive skills in identifying the topic and existing knowledge of the topic	What *exactly* is my topic about? What do I already know about this topic?
• Thinking skills such as brainstorming or concept mapping	What can I learn from other students about this topic? How might I draw a picture or concept map of what this topic is about?
• Skills in identifying print and electronic information resources	Where can I get more information about this topic? In the library? On the web?

Skills – location	Questions
• Locational skills such as the ability to find information in library catalogues, books, CD-ROMs and on the web	How will I search for the information I need? What words should I use if I use a search engine?
• Selection skills in assessing the relevance of information resources	Is this what I *really* need? Will it be useful to me?
• ICT skills using electronic sources such as the web	How do I get on to a search engine? Should I use the library website?

Skills – use	Questions
• Reading skills including the ability to skim and scan print and electronic information resources to find *relevant* information and ideas	How can I quickly decide if this is the right kind of information for me? How can I find really useful information for my topic in this book/website?
• Interactive skills including the ability to understand the content of what is being read, viewed or listened to and the ability to relate this to existing knowledge	Do I understand what I'm reading? Should I look for another source? How does this fit in with what I've already got?
• Selective skills including the ability to select the appropriate information and reject irrelevant information in the context of the above purpose	Do I really need this information? Is it relevant to my topic or is it outside my *particular* topic?
• Evaluation skills including the ability to evaluate information and ideas in relation to aspects such as the authority, reliability and currency of books, journals and websites	Who wrote this information and can I trust it? Is it biased? Is it out of date?

Figure 5.1   The PLUS model elements and student questions
(*continued on facing page*)

Recording skills including the ability to take notes in a systematic way which relates to understanding and purpose	What should I take notes on? Should I copy and paste? Will I really be able to use these notes? Have I remembered to keep a note of authors, titles etc
Synthesizing skills including the ability to bring together related ideas, facts and information about a topic and to relate these to existing knowledge	How do I bring all this together? Should I go back to my concept map? How should I organize my notes before I start to write?
Writing or presentational skills including the ability to write an essay/report/project or give a verbal presentation, in a well structured, logically ordered manner which uses the ideas and information found to good effect	How will I structure my essay or talk? Can I use my keywords or concept map? Should I read the guidelines on the library website again? Did I read the teacher's instructions correctly?
Skills – self-evaluation	**Questions**
Self-evaluation skills including the ability to reflect on the processes involved in assignment-related work and to identify areas of improvement in planning, finding information for and writing/presenting an assignment in the future	What did I learn from doing this? Did I have a good concept map? Did I search for information well? Should I have used more keywords? Did I organize my essay/talk well? Did I use the guidelines on the library website well enough? How should I do it differently next time?

Figure 5.1 (*continued*)

If a start to this process can be made in primary and secondary schools, then society as a whole will benefit. Thus there is a societal context for teaching information skills in schools as well as an educational context.

This chapter will allow teachers and school librarians to develop their own information skills and information literacy policies and practices in schools by:

- examining definitions of information skills and information literacy
- reviewing a number of key information skills models
- examining the implementation of the author's PLUS model in schools
- reviewing a number of international examples of how schools have provided information skills guidance for students
- providing examples of in-service training for information skills development in schools.

Definitions

There continues to be a debate over the terms 'information skills' and 'information literacy' and it is clear that most researchers view the term 'information literacy' as being more inclusive than 'information skills'. However, the term 'information skills' is still widely used, especially in schools when teaching students. Langford (2000) argues that Doyle's (1994) definition of information literacy should be seen as a benchmark and that information literacy can be seen as 'the ability to access, evaluate, and use information from a variety of sources, to recognise when information is needed, and to know how to learn'.

AASL/AECT's (1998) *Information Power* argues that the aim of information literacy is to 'assist all students in becoming active and creative locators, evaluators and users of information to solve problems and to satisfy their own curiosity'.

Ryan and Capra (2001) state: 'We define information literacy as the ability to process and synthesise information using the skills found in the steps of defining, locating, critically analysing and synthesising information in order to create an original response to a problem or a task.'

Herring (1996) argues: 'Information skills ... are the skills which pupils use to identify the purpose of, locate, process and communicate information concepts and ideas and then reflect upon the effective application of these skills.'

It can be argued that information literacy is a broader term, which encompasses not only skills but also attitudes to and motivation for learning; and Loertscher (2000) argues that AASL/AECT (1998) includes 'reading and enjoyment of literature' within the scope of information literacy.

Information skills models

There are several information skills models which have been designed by academics and practitioners and there is an excellent review of many of these models in Loertscher and Woolls (2002). The models selected for discussion here reflect developments in different countries but also highlight some subtle differences in approach. The aim of presenting these models is that teachers and school librarians can either adopt one model (and some schools have done this successfully) or can use elements from different models for use in their own schools.

The PLUS model

This author developed the PLUS model in 1996, and it has been used – as a whole or in part – in a number of schools in different countries. The model takes the view that students need a structure to improve their learning and their ability to produce assignments of quality in their school subjects. It is based on the processes that students go through in schools, when they are given assignments by teachers, and provides pupils with guidance that will not only help them extend their learning in curricular topics but will also, more practically, help them achieve what the teacher expects and gain higher marks.

The model consists of four interlinked steps – Purpose, Location, Use and Self-evaluation – and it is important to view these steps not as a linear process that students will always follow effortlessly, but as a circular, and sometimes repetitive, process. Self-evaluation occurs when they are asked to reflect on the effectiveness of their use of the first three steps but a student completing an assignment on the causes of the SARS outbreaks may go through the first three stages a number of times before being able to complete the fourth stage.

The PLUS model consists of a range of interlocking skills and Figure 5.1 (pages 72–3) identifies the range of skills and the questions the student might be encouraged to ask.

The most important of these skills is Purpose, because if students fail to define their purpose well, they will inevitably struggle to find the right information sources and the information they need and they may have to return to revise their purpose having gone through the Location and part of the Use stages. Thus it is worthwhile for teachers and school librarians to stress the importance of the Purpose stage to students. There has been a gradual improvement in teaching information skills in schools in recent years but teachers and school librarians must ensure that students concentrate on the Purpose and Use stages of the model and not on the Location stage which students often go straight into because they find it easier. Finding information *is* easy but finding the relevant information requires a purpose first.

The Information Search Process model

Kuhlthau's (1989) model has been one of the most influential models, and has been examined by teachers and school librarians across the world. Kuhlthau's model focuses not only on *how* students identify purpose and find and use information but also on *what* students feel about the process. Figure 5.2 shows

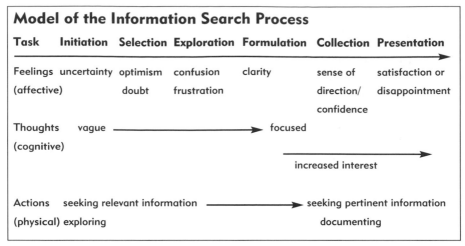

Figure 5.2 Kuhlthau's Information Search Process model

how Kuhlthau's model traces the students' progress, from uncertainty about what they are trying to accomplish in the early stages of doing an assignment through to the more confident approach taken near the end of the process. What this model demonstrates is that students who perform more effectively at the Task Initiation (Purpose in the PLUS model) stage will experience less ambiguity and will feel more confident at an earlier stage in the process.

The Big Six model

This model is the most widely known and used information skills model in North America. The stages in the model of Eisenberg and Berkowitz (1988) are:

- Task definition (determining the purpose and need for information)
- Information seeking strategies (examining alternative approaches to acquiring the appropriate information to meet defined needs)
- Location and access (locating information sources and information within sources)
- Use of information (using a source to gain information)
- Synthesis (integrating information drawn from a range of sources)
- Evaluation (making judgements based on a set of criteria).

The Big Six model is similar to the PLUS model in emphasizing the importance of purpose at the start of the process and self-evaluation at the end of it.

The ILPO model

This model, developed by Ryan and Capra (2001) has been widely used in Australia, and the materials have been adapted for publication in North America. The steps in the ILPO model are:

- Defining: The stage of formulating questions, analysing and clarifying the requirements of the problem or task...
- Locating: Following the defining stage, the student identifies potential sources of information and is able to locate and access a variety of resources using multiple formats.
- Selecting/Analysing: The student analyses, selects and rejects information appropriate to the problem or task from the located resources....
- Organizing/Synthesizing: In this stage, the student critically analyses and organises the gathered information, synthesises new learning incorporating prior knowledge and develops original solutions to a problem or task....
- Creating/Presenting: The student creates an original response to the problem or task, presenting the solution to an appropriate audience...
- Evaluation: In the final stage, the student critically evaluates the effectiveness of his or her ability to complete the requirements of the task and identifies future learning needs.

The authors of the ILPO model stress the need to encourage students to regard the process as one where they engage in critical thinking in order to come up with original responses to tasks or problems; therefore, teachers and school librarians need to ensure that the types of assignments students are given will develop these skills.

Clearly, the above models share certain common elements: they all stress the need for students to be involved in thinking about the *process* of doing an assignment or solving a problem as well as thinking about its *content*. As will be seen below – in the use of the PLUS model in schools – students are quite capable, even at the age of 10 or 11, of responding to questions about identifying purpose or locating and using information and they *are* able to reflect on how they might improve their own approach. Therefore, teachers and school librarians would benefit from building in self-evaluation elements into assignment and project guidelines, as this would not only encourage students to reflect on their own work but would also provide excellent feedback to teachers. This in turn could help in the development of new and more effective assignments.

Using the PLUS model in schools

The PLUS model has been used and adapted in a number of schools in different countries. In the UK, two research studies have been carried out at Ripon Grammar School in Yorkshire. The studies were done by the author, the school librarian, Anne-Marie Tarter, and Simon Naylor, a physics teacher. The two studies looked at how the PLUS model was used by year 7 (11 to 12-year-old) and year 8 (12 to 13-year-old) students who were completing projects in Earth and Space (year 7) and Sound Technology (year 8). The students were given an introduction to the PLUS model ('Planning' was used instead of 'Purpose' with these students) as well as guidance on brainstorming, selecting resources, note-taking and presentation, both written and verbal. As part of the assignment they also completed self-evaluation questionnaires which asked them about the processes they followed in doing it, and the extent to which having the PLUS model was beneficial. Altogether, 140 students took part in the two studies. The results show that the students were overwhelmingly positive about their use of the PLUS model as a tool which helped them to plan their assignment better, to search for and find more relevant information, to take notes in a more organized manner and to organize their written work and verbal presentation in a more structured way.

In both projects conducted by Herring, Tarter and Naylor (2000), students used group brainstorming to explore their existing knowledge of the general topic, e.g. Earth and Space, and to select their individual or group topic. The students (student comments in parentheses) viewed brainstorming in a positive way as it helped them to:

- share ideas ('We shared ideas and found out what we didn't know from other people.')
- collect more ideas/information ('We collected more answers as some people might know more about one thing and others about other things.')
- work as a team ('asking the questions and working and co-operating like a team')

- know what to look for at the next stage ('because we knew what information we had and what we needed to find out').

The students also commented on the negative aspects of brainstorming, which related more to *behaviour* than to the content of discussion, e.g. arguments in the group and the bossiness of some group members.

Students also had to devise a concept map, which they referred to as a spider diagram, for each project; they were very positive, saying that using a concept map helped them to:

- form questions ('Using keywords [from the concept map] helped us to form questions and find the information.')
- identify and organize information ('I was able to sort out what I know from what I didn't, and find out what I needed to research.')

When asked about locating information, the students mostly agreed that using keywords from both the brainstorming and concept-mapping stages was beneficial, as it focused their minds on what to search for ('because you knew what to look for and not worry about what information to use'), and it helped them to reject irrelevant information ('Because you only had useful information and not non-useful').

Students were taught about different ways of taking notes, e.g. note cards or spider diagrams, using a number of different strategies. When asked *how* they chose what to take notes on, their responses included:

- most relevant, useful or interesting; or simply best information ('I take notes on things when I know they will be useful for my topic.')
- information related to keywords ('use words/phrases that link with or are about your topic')
- skim-read and choose relevant information ('I skim-read and pick out the keywords for my topic.').

The students were asked how they decided what should be in the group's written report in the Earth and Space project and it was encouraging that 44% used the brainstorming sheets which they had completed earlier and 44% used keywords from their concept maps.

When asked about how effective their use of the PLUS model had been, students commented on the following areas:

- planning ('It is extremely helpful and it is a good way of planning what you're going to do because it would be quite difficult if you didn't do much planning.')
- stages ('I think PLUS works well and you don't miss out any stages in researching the information.')
- being organized ('I thought it helped as it kept us organized.')
- reflection ('It makes you think and look at the information you have. It makes you make lots of decisions and then look back on your decisions once you have finished. I think it is a very useful and a good system.')
- transfer of skills/future use ('PLUS is very helpful because you remember it and you do the same method every time you do project work.').

The overall conclusions from both projects, based on the students' questionnaire responses and interviews with the school librarian and the teacher, were that the students benefited from the structure that the PLUS model had provided, from working more independently, and from having to reflect on their own work. The teacher and school librarian commented that the students' work had improved and that they now took more care to develop their work further and were less inclined to copy. It is clear that the students benefited from using the PLUS model in this school but it is also clear that providing students with another model may well have had the same results. Therefore, teachers and school librarians should view these studies not in relation to whether the PLUS model is better than other models but in relation to the benefits gained from providing students with a clear structure.

Information skills and web resources: searching for information

Schools across the world are placing more importance on incorporating the use of the web into their information skills and literacy programmes and many are including advice on using the web in their school websites. The following examples show a range of approaches which teachers and school librarians may wish to study and adapt to their own situation. There is no *one* way of teaching students about using the web. Some schools prefer to provide students with a mixture of advice and links to sites which have the school's approval. Figure 5.3 shows advice given to high school students in the Mesquite Independent School District.

A Web Directory...
- has a structure that can be browsed
- is built by human editors who categorize web pages based on their content
- is similar to the table of contents in a book
- is good to use when...
  you are a 'newbie' on the Net
  you are looking for a list of web sites compiled by an 'expert'
  you want to see what's 'hot'
  you have a general topic in mind and need some help narrowing it down

A Search Engine...
- must be searched with a keyword
- runs an automated program that searches the Internet for web pages containing your keyword
- gives you results based on how many times your keyword appeared in a page
- is similar to the index in a book
- is good to use when...
  you are looking for a very specific topic
  you want to combine keywords

A Metasearch Engine...
- sends your keyword(s) out to several search engines at once
- blends the results of the search together on one page
- is good to use when...
  you need a few good links *fast*

Figure 5.3   Advice on searching for high school students in Mesquite Independent School District, Mesquite, TX, USA
(http://www.mesquiteisd.org/library/hstools.htm)

Students in this school are then directed towards recommended sites, as seen in Figure 5.4.

A different approach is taken by Melbourne High School who require students to examine a list of online and web-related skills and to have a teacher verify completion of the skills. Figure 5.5 shows the skills highlighted and clearly demonstrates how web-related skills are seen as part of information skills in this school, with the reference to the 'Research Process'.

St Joseph's Nudgee College provides more specific advice on its school library website to students learning to search for information on the web. Figure 5.6 shows a section from the web-searching pages.

Further examples of how schools approach teaching web-related searching skills and how they relate these skills to the overall information skills programme of the school will be provided in Chapter 6.

Figure 5.4 Links provided for high school students in Mesquite
Independent School District, Mesquite, TX, USA
(http://www.mesquiteisd.org/library/hstools.htm)

Information skills and web resources: evaluating websites

Teaching students how to evaluate information found in print or electronic
sources of information is a key aspect of information skills teaching. The intention here is to examine how selected schools have provided guidance for their
students in relation to evaluating websites and what activities students might
be given to provide them with an understanding of the importance of website
evaluation. Figure 5.7 (page 85) is an example of part of one school's guidance
to students on evaluating websites and takes the form of a number of questions
which the students might ask when deciding on the quality of a website.

A briefer but still effective approach is taken by Westminster School and
Figure 5.8 (page 86) is a good example of how students can be encouraged to
critically appraise websites before using them.

An innovative approach to advising students about the importance of website evaluation is taken by Lovett School Libraries and this can be seen in
Figure 5.9 (page 87), where students are posed a number of key questions.

An excellent example of how to teach students to evaluate websites is provided by Valenza (2001) who encourages teachers to take a proactive approach
by presenting students with a task that will test their evaluative powers and
encourage critical thinking when they analyse websites. Figure 5.10 shows an
extract from a proposed lesson.

The On-line Searching Checklist
There are many different sources of information on-line as well as the Internet. CD ROMs on the Melbourne High School network include *Encyclopaedia Britannica*, *The Age*, *The Australian Year Book* and the *McGraw-Hill Encyclopaedia of Science and Technology*. The library catalogue is also a source of on-line information.

To get the best information when you search you need to develop the skills listed in the table below.

- Check through the list and identify the skills you have and the skills you need.
- Put the date when you have mastered a new skill.
- Have your subject teacher initial the skill when you have an example of your work that demonstrates your skills.

On-line searching skills	Skills I have	Date	Teacher's Initials
'browse' searching			
• recognising when to expect information to be displayed in alphabetical order (e.g. a list of authors, or Encarta search)			
• knowing how to move backwards and forwards in a hierarchical subject structure (e.g. a directory like Yahoo!)			
• recognising when a browse search will be the most efficient tool to use (e.g. when you are beginning a topic)			
keyword searching			
• knowing how to choose appropriate keywords (ref. Research Process checklist)			
• knowing how to apply Boolean Logic to refine a search (refer to the MHS Library homepage)			
specifically Internet searching			
• knowing how to search for an exact phrase			
• knowing how to search for an image			
• using different search engines for different purposes			
• scanning results to interpret the URL (e.g. Where does the information originate?)			

Figure 5.5   The Online Searching Checklist from Melbourne High School, Australia (www.mhs.vic.edu.au/home/library)

Subject Definition
- A major part of planning a search is defining the subject you are looking for.
- This involves thinking about the subject you are researching.
- It is best, when Internet searching to *identify all the words that can be used for the subject being searched for*.
- For example, if you wanted to locate information on jails, you would also possibly search for – prisons, penitentiaries, law, crime or punishment.

Case Sensitive Search Tools
- If you type in a search term in capitals, the search tool will only look for items that are capitalised.
- It is better therefore to *search using an uncapitalised form* so as to increase the probability of retrieving relevant keywords.

Phrase Searching
- If you are **searching for a phrase, enclose the phrase in quotation marks, ""**.
- For example, "capital punishment".

Truncation
- *Use an asterisk (*) to locate alternate forms of a search term*.
- For example, if you are trying to locate information about gardens, you could type in garden*. This would result in the search tool looking for terms relating to garden, gardens, gardening, gardener and gardeners.

Boolean Logic
- Boolean logic is a system whereby certain words can be used within a search string to *widen* or narrow searches.

Widening Searches
- *OR or* -
Looks for the occurrence of either of the two nominated terms in the website, e.g.
Type – college or university
COLLEGE
UNIVERSITY

Figure 5.6   Searching tips for students at St Joseph's Nudgee College, Australia (www.nudgee.com/library/)

In-service training

As information literacy is now regarded as a key element in a student's education, it is important that all school staff are encouraged to think about the following:

- What are information skills and why are they important?

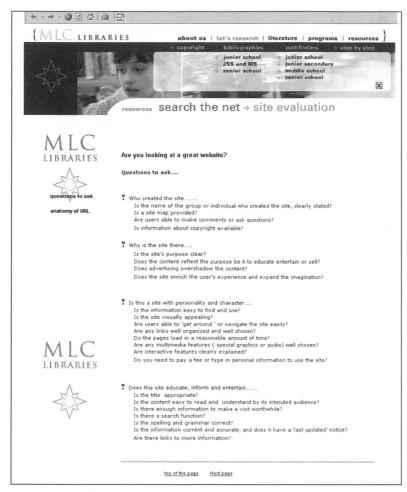

Figure 5.7 Guidance on evaluating websites from Methodist Ladies College, Melbourne, Australia (from school intranet)

- Who teaches information skills in the school?
- What information skills do students need when using the web?
- To what extent have the school's teachers and school librarian thought about their *own* information skills?
- How can students be provided with guidance on information skills on the school website?

All the above topics might serve as the basis for an in-service training day, but

---

Evaluating Webpages
* ***Identify the purpose of the webpage***
  Is it commercial, educational, entertainment?
  Is it free or are there hidden costs? For example, advertisements?
  Is it produced for general philanthropic reasons or egotism, or is someone
  pushing a narrow, subjective argument?
  Why is the page there at all?
  Who has an interest in maintaining or producing such a site?

* ***Identify who the intended audience is***
  Is it:
  a) a journal article available for general sale to the public
  OR
  b) a lecture given to postgraduate students at x university on animal
     photoperiodism?

* ***Assess the reputation/authority of the site***
  Who has written it?
  * a company with vested interests?
  * a recognised higher education institution? OR
  * Chad D Jr. from Nowhereville, Arkansas?

* ***Find how up-to-date the site is***
  Check for the date that the site/page was last updated. It is usually listed at the
  top or bottom of the page e.g. on the Library webpages.

Figure 5.8   Advice on evaluating websites from Westminster School, London, UK
(http://library.westminster.org.uk/Info/information_seeking_strategy.htm)

this section will focus on examples relating to information skills and the web.

One very successful in-service training session, which this author has run in a number of countries, relates to reading websites. The focus of this session is to ask teachers and school librarians to examine their own information skills in relation to the use of websites. How do they as individuals 'read' a website? How do they navigate the site to find the information they need? How do they evaluate what they are reading? How do they take notes? By answering these questions, teachers and school librarians can then take a more carefully thought out approach to teaching students how to use websites effectively. Figure 5.11 (page 89) shows the content of the workshop.

Those teachers and librarians who attended the in-service session were asked to fill in a questionnaire, shown in Figure 5.12 (page 90).

Analysis of the questionnaires shows that there was a wide range of views on

'If it's on the web is it true?'

Here are some questions everyone should consider when relying on information collected from the web. A lot of this you would think is common sense. Certainly it's an approach we should use with any information resource, but especially with the Internet we need to start becoming critical consumers of information.

- **Who?** Qui? Wer? ¿Quién?
  Who is responsible for the information? A Ph.D., a first-year university student, a high school teacher, a 6th grader, a salesman, a cult member, a pedophile, a royalist, a republican, a democrat, an anarchist, a Unitarian, a Catholic priest? Is there a name on the page? Does the author have credentials/expertise in the relevant subject?

- **Where?** D'où? Woher? ¿De dónde?
  Where does the information come from? Is it from a university, an elementary school, a personal computer in someone's home, a commercial enterprise, a political group, a religious group, an industrialized nation, a developing nation, a democratic nation, a totalitarian nation?

- **Why?** Pourquoi? Warum? ¿Por qué?
  Why does this material appear on the web? What is its purpose? — to instruct, to convince, to sell you something, to convert, to mislead, to entrap? Is it biased or distorted? Is this the only view?

- **What?** Quoi? Was? ¿Qué?
  What is the best place to look for the info I need? Is the web the best/easiest/quickest place to find the answer to my question? Is the information supported/corroborated by info in my textbook, library books, magazine articles? What comparisons can be made to other sources? Am I saving time by using the web?

- **How?** Comment? Wie? ¿Cómo?
  How is the information formatted? How easy is it to read? How well is it written? Is it full of spelling and stylistic errors? How does it rate for age-appropriateness? Does it require background information that I do not have?

- **When?** Quand? Wann? ¿Cuándo?
  When was the page written? When was it last updated? Is it still valid? Is it out of date? Do the links go anywhere? Will I be able to access the page tomorrow, next week, next month?

Figure 5.9   Advice for students at Lovett School Libraries, Atlanta, GA, USA
(www.lovett.org/libraryweb.library.htm)

- **Introduction**
If you are like most students, you are relying heavily on resources from the Web for your research. Not all Web resources are created equal. If fact, there are great variations in the quality of the resources you access. The rule of thumb is 'when in doubt, doubt.' When you carefully select your resources, when you understand their strengths and limits, you create better products.

- **The Task**
You will be working in groups of four to evaluate a group of Web pages on the topic of tobacco and smoking, or cloning or another topic of your teacher's choice. Each of you will be examining sites from a different perspective. You will be ranking the sites and comparing your rankings with the rest of the class.

- **Resources**
You will each be responsible for completing an evaluation chart, focusing on the perspective you assume within your group.

Figure 5.10 A lesson on evaluating websites for students in grades 9 to 12
(http://mciu.org/~spjvweb/evalwebstu.html)

some aspects of reading for information on websites. There was general agreement on the use of keywords, paragraph headings and graphics titles when skimming and scanning as well as general agreement on evaluating content, e.g. authority, level of language, use of graphics and up-to-date-ness. However, in relation to Question 1, about understanding, responses ranged from looking in a book or encyclopaedia in the library, to asking a person for help or seeking out another website, web-based dictionary or encyclopaedia. There was extensive discussion in some groups as to whether they would seek understanding *away from* the computer and this raised the question of whether using websites is likely to make users forget about print resources. This point was seen as important in relation to students who often see the web as the *only* source of information they need for assignments.

In relation to note-taking, there was also a wide range of methods used. These included 'traditional' note-taking (writing notes by hand), although there was also a range of styles here, from lists to quotations to concept maps. Many teachers and school librarians preferred to use the computer to take notes: styles included cutting and pasting into a Microsoft® Word™ document, using Notepad to write notes, printing and highlighting. In relation to advising students, there was again a range of views in that some teachers and librarians advised students *against* cutting and pasting, while

---

Reading for information and note-taking: websites

Seminar for teachers and school librarians

Aims
This seminar aims to:

- ask teachers and school librarians to reflect on their own information skills strategies when using websites
- discuss ways in which this experience can be passed on to students
- provide ideas for INSET with teachers in the participant's own school.

Methodology
1. Each teacher or librarian will look at the following site and think about the questions on the back of this sheet: http://quake.wr.usgs.gov – click on **Hazards and Preparedness**, then – **When will the next great quake strike Northern California?**
2. Participants will split into groups of four or five.
3. Each seminar participant will complete the questions on the back of this sheet individually (no conferring!).
4. Each group will then read each other's responses and identify two similarities and two differences of approach.
5. The group will then be asked to make two recommendations in relation to:
   - How can the teacher's and/or the school librarian's experience be used as an example with pupils?
   - Could this session be replicated in INSET sessions with other teachers in your school?
6. Discussion and questions.

Figure 5.11 Outline of in-service training session on reading websites

others were content to let students cut and paste but with the proviso that students understood that they could not just copy this straight into their assignments. In some school libraries, printing by students is restricted, partly to save costs but also, in some schools, to encourage pupils to read from the screen and take notes either in writing or using a Word™ document. Overall, this in-service session raised many questions and generated many ideas for both teachers and school librarians at sessions in the UK, Belgium, Portugal and Lithuania.

Conclusion

Information literacy is now regarded by governments across the world as a

Reading for information and note-taking: websites

Seminar for teachers and school librarians

Assume that you are reading for information in an academic context, e.g. for an assignment, so that you are doing the same as your pupils/students do when reading for information. One part of your assignment is about the 1906 Californian Earthquake and predictions about future earthquakes. The website you are using is one of the resources recommended. You are doing this part of the assignment in the school library.

Questions

1. How do you make sure that you understand what you are reading? What do you do if you don't understand something on the web page?

2. How do you skim screens of text and graphics to get an overall impression?

3. How do you scan screens of text and graphics to find particular information?

4. How do you evaluate the source you are using (i.e. the website)?

5. How do you take notes from the website in relation to your original purpose?

Figure 5.12 Questionnaire filled in by in-service trainees at session shown in Fig. 5.11

core educational and life skill, and schools have a key role to play in developing their students' information literacy. By studying the theory and practice examined in this chapter, teachers and school librarians will be able to examine their own information skills and then develop programmes in the school which will encourage the development of information skills in students. There is now an ever-increasing emphasis on skills related to the use of web resources and it is important that students learn the skills of identifying and evaluating web resources, but only in the context of their identified *purpose*. Web-related skills must, therefore, be seen as part of the whole information skills process: by using a model such as the author's PLUS model, teachers and school librarians can provide students with the support and structure they need when using print and electronic resources in their assignments.

References

AASL/AECT (1998) *Information Power: building partnerships for learning*, Chicago, IL, ALA.

Doyle, C. (1994) *Information Literacy in an Information Society*, ERIC Clearing House on Information and Technology.

Eisenberg, M. and Berkowitz, R. (1988) *Information Problem Solving: the Big Six approach to library and information skills instruction*, Ablex, www.big6.com.

Herring, J. (1996) *Teaching Information Skills in Schools*, London, Library Assocation Publishing.

Herring, J., Tarter, A.-M. and Naylor, S. (2002) An Evaluation of the Use of the PLUS Model to Develop Pupils' Information Skills in a Secondary School, *School Libraries Worldwide*, **8** (1) (January), 1–24.

Kuhlthau, C. (1989) Information Search Process, *School Library Media Quarterly*, **22** (1) Fall, 19–25, www.scils.rutgers.edu/~kuhlthau/Search%20Process.htm.

Langford, L. (2000) Information Literacy? Seeking clarification. In Howe, E. (ed.), *Developing Information Literacy*, IASL/LMC Source.

Loertscher, D. (2000) *Taxonomies of the School Library Media Program*, 2nd edn, Spring, TX, Hi Willow Research and Publishing.

Loertscher, D. and Woolls, B. (2002) *Information Literacy: a review of the research*, 2nd edn, Spring, TX, Hi Willow Research and Publishing.

Ryan, J. and Capra, S. (2001) Information Literacy Planning for Educators: the ILPO approach, *School Libraries Worldwide*, 7 (1) (January), 1–10, www.aber-ac.uk/tfpl/elibs/s/worldwide.asp.

Valenza, J. (2001) *A Webquest about Evaluating Websites*, http://mciu.org/~spjvweb/evalwebstu.html.

6

The PLUS model and the web

···
Having read this chapter, you will be able to:

- use the PLUS model when teaching students how to use the web and other resources
- improve your students' use of the web through their use of brainstorming and concept mapping
- improve your students' use of the web through their use of keywords in searching for information
- improve your students' skills in reading websites and taking notes
- improve your students' use of the web in writing and presenting
- teach your students how to evaluate their own use of the web and other resources
- develop an in-service training session based on the PLUS model.
···

Introduction

The PLUS model can be seen as an example of how to develop information literacy amongst students in schools. Todd (2003) argues that information literacy 'is about the systematic and explicit provision of a range of intellectual scaffolds for effective engagement and utilisation of information in all its forms (electronic, print, popular culture) and for constructing sense, understanding and new knowledge'.

Barrett and Danks (2003) state that '"Scaffolding" is providing a structure for students that will support their learning and their application of skills.'

As was seen in Chapter 5, the PLUS model can provide students with a positive and easy-to-understand structure or scaffold which they can use to enhance their learning when doing assignments. The PLUS model has been used in schools to focus students' attention on the need for careful use of the web for finding and using information. One of the problems faced by teachers and school librarians across the world is that students often use the web in the *same* way that they use books and CD-ROMs. The problem lies in the fact that the web is so much bigger and less reliable than the school library catalogue, books and CD-ROMs. A student searching the library catalogue or a CD-ROM for information about the causes of earthquakes can be reasonably sure that using the search terms **earthquake** and **causes** will not result in thousands of hits. Similarly, using a book index will take the student to a limited number of sources of information. Therefore, students have to be taught that using the web requires a *different* approach in some ways. The main differences will be that students will have to define their searches more clearly, to be more selective in their choice of websites found and to realize that websites, unlike books and CD-ROMs chosen for the school library, are *not* mediated by a teacher or school librarian.

All four elements of the PLUS model – Purpose, Location, Use and Self-Evaluation – need to be used by students whether they are using print or electronic sources of information, but some aspects need to be emphasized more when students use the web. This chapter will highlight the use of the PLUS model in three UK schools, providing teachers and school librarians with a practical guide to using the model when teaching students about using the web. In particular:

- encouraging students to use brainstorming and concept mapping in defining purpose
- improving students' searching skills in locating information
- developing students' reading skills, note-taking skills and writing/presenting skills when using information
- showing students the benefits of self-evaluation
- developing in-service sessions for using the PLUS model in schools.

Examples from schools using similar approaches will also be provided.

Purpose

One of the most common criticisms that teachers make about student assignments is that the student has not focused clearly on the topic and that this has led to an assignment which is not well thought-out, well researched or well organized. This can often be due to the fact that the student has not clearly identified what the purpose of their assignment is. Teachers and school librarians seek to encourage critical thinking in their students by presenting them with assignments where students are guided to some extent but are also given some freedom of choice. McKenzie's (2000) Questioning Toolkit is a useful place for teachers and school librarians to start to look for ideas on how to encourage student learning by allowing students to impose their own questions in relation to topics they research for assignments.

One important aspect of questioning for students is for them to ask about the *purpose* of their assignment, with questions such as:

- What is it that I am being asked to do?
- What is my assignment *really* about?
- What is my assignment *not* about?
- What do I already know about my topic?

At St Ivo School, students are encouraged to brainstorm questions relating to a Religious Education project before going on to use websites selected and evaluated by the teacher and the school librarian. Figure 6.1 shows part of an intranet website used by students doing this project.

At Ripon Grammar School, students use the PLUS model from their first year at the school (year 7, age 11–12) until they leave. In this school, 'Purpose' is replaced by 'Planning' because students preferred this term. Figure 6.2 shows the first part of the guidelines provided to students when starting an assignment.

Brainstorm: What do you know? Find your keywords

Q. Who goes on Hajj?   Q. Where do pilgrims go on
_____   Hajj?_____

_____   _____

Q. From what religion does this come?

_____

Web-site addresses for working at home:
http://islamicity.com/mosque/hajj/
www.geocities.com/TheTropics/Cabana/7086/hajj.html
http://channel4.com/life/microsites/H/hajj/index.html

Figure 6.1   Brainstorming advice to students at St Ivo School, Cambridgeshire, UK

PLANNING my work

NAME _____ FORM _____

My topic is _____

My research is for what purpose? (What do you need to produce from the information you find?)

My work must include: (How much information do you need? In what format, i.e. do you need pictures, etc.?)

My final written work will be written for what audience? (At what level will you need your information to be?)

How much time do I have to do this work ?
        My research must be completed by _____. My final written work must be completed by _____.
        I will have _____ lessons and ___ homeworks to complete this work.

My work must be ___ word processed ___ hand written ___ either word processed or hand written.

I must remember that I will be marked on my research notes as well as my final product.

Figure 6.2   Guidance to students starting an assignment at Ripon Grammar School, North Yorkshire, UK

This encourages students to think about the *process* that they are about to go through and not just about the content of the assignment. Students are then encouraged to write down what they know about their topic and to brainstorm the topic by themselves or with other students. One of the outcomes of this brainstorming is a concept map.

Concept mapping is now accepted as a tried and tested method which can be used by both teachers and students. Conlon (2002) states that concept maps

PLANNING: Part Three, How can I ORGANISE my ideas?

Look at your brainstorming and think of how you can group your ideas into
MAIN HEADINGS. You may decide to omit some ideas and you may think of
others as you work. You are aiming to identify the main topics you will wish to
cover in your final text.

Put the main subject in the middle and add your Main Headings on the ends of
the arms. **Add other arms and topic circles as needed.**

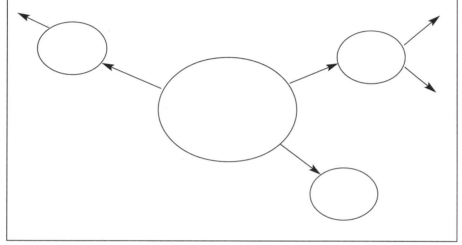

Figure 6.3   Concept map from Ripon Grammar School, North Yorkshire, UK

'are powerful classroom tools which can be used by teachers and pupils. ...
Pupils can create ... [concept] maps for purposes that include summarising
subject matter, supporting discussion and reflection, and recording and planning independent study.'

Conlon also notes that concept maps encourage students to learn 'transferable thinking skills'. At Ripon Grammar School, students are provided with
what Conlon calls a '*Tabula Rasa* ("blank slate")[which] involves the creation
of a map from scratch'. Figure 6.3 shows an example of a blank concept map.

Conlon also alludes to: 'Scaffolded mapping tasks ... in which elements of
the map are provided by the teacher, leaving the learner to supply the rest. The
intention is to provide support (certainly to prevent floundering) and constrain
the learner's thinking to "productive" directions.'

At the Jack Hunt School, which also uses the PLUS model at all levels of

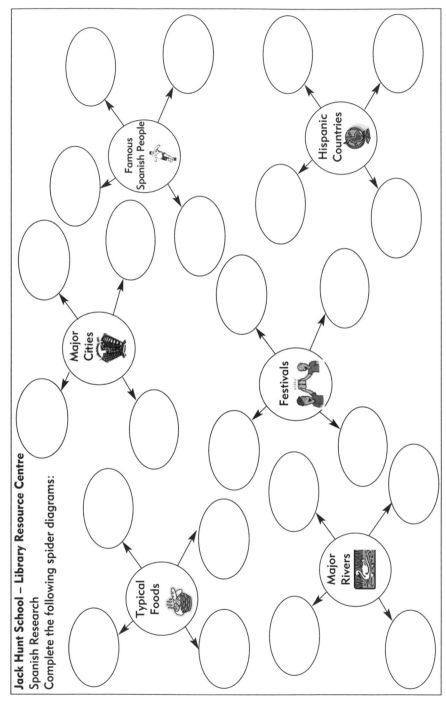

Jack Hunt School – Library Resource Centre
Spanish Research
Complete the following spider diagrams:

Typical Foods

Major Rivers

Festivals

Major Cities

Famous Spanish People

Hispanic Countries

Figure 6.4 Scaffolded concept map from Jack Hunt School, Cambridgeshire, UK

the school, scaffolded mapping is used as part of the Purpose stage for students. Figure 6.4 shows an example used with students doing a project on Spain.

The final part of Purpose is for students to identify keywords from concept maps or lists of questions. Figure 6.5 from Ripon Grammar School combines these two elements.

A similar approach to this element of the PLUS model is taken by Gladstone Secondary School, Canada, where students are provided with a useful checklist which will help them to identify a clear purpose. Figure 6.6 shows this checklist.

From these examples, it can be seen that teachers and school librarians will improve their students' learning skills, including mapping skills, questioning skills and planning skills, by focusing students' attention on identifying a clear purpose for their assignment. It will be seen in the rest of this chapter how crucial Purpose is to the information skills process, as all other actions taken by students relate back to this initial step. Students who go straight to searching the web without a clear purpose are doomed to failure and frustration as the results of their searching may well be mostly irrelevant to their topic.

ASKING QUESTIONS: Now that you have worked out what you know about your topic, it is time to decide what exactly you need to research. So ... what do you need to find out??? This is a very important step as asking the right questions will guide you in choosing the best resources and finding information quickly and effectively. Aim for 5-7 good questions.

1.

2.

3.

4.

5.

6.

7.

Can you think of any KEYWORDS to use to look for in the index of a book or on a Search Engine search window?

Figure 6.5   Student questioning from Ripon Grammar School, North Yorkshire, UK

THE RESEARCH QUEST: STUDENT CHECKLIST

Name: _____ Teacher: _____ Block: ____

Assignment: _____

FOCUS

TO **FOCUS** MY RESEARCH PROJECT, I have identified:

- ☐ My research challenge and my purpose
- ☐ Critical questions
- ☐ My audience
- ☐ What I already know and what I need to know
- ☐ What my product might be
- ☐ A plan for my time

FIND AND FILTER

TO **FIND AND FILTER** RESOURCES FOR RESEARCH, I:

- ☐ Located different resources (print and electronic)
- ☐ Decided which resources might be suitable
- ☐ Selected the most appropriate resources
- ☐ Revised my research questions (if necessary)

WORK WITH INFORMATION

TO **WORK WITH THE INFORMATION** I FOUND, I have:

- ☐ Read (viewed, listened to) the information
- ☐ Interpreted, recorded, and organized
- ☐ Looked for patterns and made connections
- ☐ Checked that I understand the information
- ☐ Reviewed, revised, reorganized, edited

COMMUNICATE

TO **COMMUNICATE** THE RESULTS OF MY WORK, I have:

- ☐ Prepared my final results
- ☐ Shared my new ideas, knowledge, or product
- ☐ Acted on the findings

REFLECT

TO **REFLECT** ON THE RESEARCH I UNDERTOOK, I have:

- ☐ Decided what I have learned about the topic
- ☐ Determined what I did that worked well
- ☐ Figured out what I will do differently next time
- ☐ Reviewed what I have learned about researching

Based on model developed by BCTLA and adopted by the Ministry of Education, January 2001

© Gladstone Secondary School Library 2002-2003

Figure 6.6 Student checklist from Gladstone Secondary School, Canada
(http://gladstone.vsb.bc.ca/library/infolit/RESQUEST%20checklist.doc)

Location

There has been much attention in schools across the world recently on providing students with ICT (Information and Communication Technology) skills and part of this has been focused on teaching students how to search the web. For most students, searching the web is no more difficult than using the school library catalogue or a CD-ROM. However, for most students, searching the web *effectively* is a much more difficult task, in terms of retrieving relevant information. Examples of teaching students how to effectively locate and evaluate sources from the web were provided in Chapter 5. The following examples demonstrate how the Location step in the PLUS model can help students to become more skilled web users by teaching them not only how to find sources but how to evaluate web sources before going on to the Use step in the PLUS model.

Figure 6.7 shows a page from the St Ivo School intranet which students use to access information when doing project work. The page focuses on Location but students have links to the other elements of the PLUS model on the page.

Similar advice on searching is provided at Kinnick High School, Japan,

Figure 6.7   Location advice to students at St Ivo School, Cambridgeshire, UK

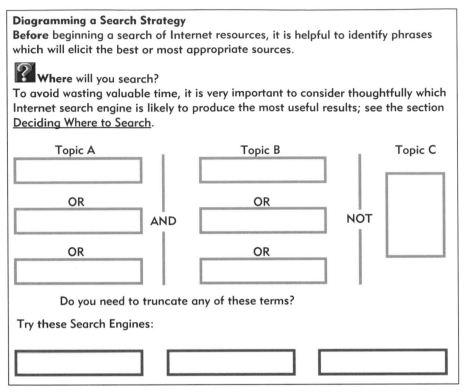

Figure 6.8   Search strategy advice for students at Kinnick High School, Japan
(www.surfline.ne.jp/janetm/diagram.html)

where students are provided with a scaffold to help them formulate their web search, as shown in Figure 6.8.

Ripon Grammar School's Location advice to students also includes a requirement within an assignment (e.g. Sound Technology) to review print and electronic information resources before selecting the most appropriate sources. Figure 6.9 shows part of the material provided to students and asks them to review books and websites.

At Jack Hunt School, students are provided with scaffolding in the form of a table which students complete when evaluating pre-selected websites. Figure 6.10 (page 104) shows an example of this.

The 'Location' aspect of the PLUS model achieves two main results for students. On the positive side, students who clearly identify a purpose, identify keywords and use these to search for information on the web, are likely to find relevant materials. On the negative side, students who have failed to identify a

LOCATING the best information for your purpose

You need to compare a variety of resources until you decide which are the BEST ONES for YOUR PURPOSE.
        LOOK AT A COLLECTION OF BOOKS, CD-ROMS, INTERNET SITES
(You will need to look at at least 6 in total)
- Can you find out anything in the book about the author? The publisher? and why they wrote the book (website, etc)?
- When was it published?
- Can you find the information you need easily? (index, contents, headings, pictures) Is there enough information on your topic?
- Can you understand the information? Is it written at your level?
- Does it ANSWER YOUR QUESTIONS?

> AUTHOR:
> TITLE OF THE RESOURCE:
> DATE OF PUBLICATION:
> PUBLISHER AND PLACE OF PUBLICATION:
>
> USING YOUR KEYWORDS, SCAN THE CONTENTS AND THE INDEX AND MAKE A NOTE OF ANY USEFUL PAGES
>
> _____
>
> SKIM READ ONE OF THE RELEVANT PAGES. CAN YOU UNDERSTAND IT? Yes _____ No _____
>
> I WILL _____ WILL NOT _____ USE THIS RESOURCE.
> GIVE YOUR REASONS WHY:

Figure 6.9   Reviewing print and electronic sources at Ripon Grammar School, North Yorkshire, UK

clear purpose are unlikely to find relevant information and will therefore have to return to the Purpose stage. For some students, this is a salutary experience and they can learn from their mistakes. It also demonstrates that the PLUS model can be an iterative one for students, in that they may have to return to Purpose in order to define their purpose and ask relevant questions. This

Evaluating a website – Can you trust it?
The internet is a fantastic resource to research a topic like fox hunting. However, you need to be very careful!

Anyone can put information on the internet.

Not everyone checks facts or tries to give balanced information.

You need to learn how to judge whether you can trust the information that you find.

Using the list of URLs provided, analyse the websites to find out whether you would regard them as biased or not.

URL and Name of Organisation responsible for site	How well is the site written? Is it easy to read or difficult to understand?	How does the website use images? Photographs? Video Clips? Clip Art? **WHY?**	Are there any other types of information available? Press Clippings? Links to other sites? **WHY?**	Can you contact the author of the site or any relevant organisation?	Does the site set out to inform you or persuade you? <u>Explain how you reached your decisions.</u>

Figure 6.10   Evaluating websites at Jack Hunt School, Cambridgeshire, UK

FIND AND FILTER	**TO FIND AND FILTER RESOURCES FOR RESEARCH, I:**
	☐ Located different resources (print and electronic)
	☐ Decided which resources might be suitable
	☐ Selected the most appropriate resources
	☐ Revised my research questions (if necessary)

Figure 6.11   Finding information at Gladstone Secondary School, Canada
(http://gladstone.vsb.bc.ca/library/infolit/RESQUEST%20checklist.doc)

process is neatly shown in Figure 6.11 from Gladstone Secondary School.

Use

As was shown in Chapter 5, the Use aspect of the PLUS model relates to how effectively students use information once they locate it in print or electronic sources and this involves a range of skills including skimming and scanning,

---

USING INFORMATION RESOURCES EFFECTIVELY

From the resources you have evaluated,

CHOOSE THE BEST THREE TO START WITH
(use the others only if you have time)

Whether you use a computer, a book, a person, or a newspaper, you need to be able to:

- Use your KEYWORDS to SCAN the Table of Contents, Indexes, Chapter Headings, Pictures and Diagrams to find appropriate information
- STAY FOCUSED on your questions while you SKIM read the text. Does it answer your questions? If not, move on.
- If your mind starts to wander…go back to your questions and keywords. They are your best guides!

When you find the information you need, you will want to record it for use later on. There are several different ways of recording information. Tick the one which you are directed to use this time:

___ Note cards
___ Spider diagram
___ Grid
___ Tape recording
___ Computer database or wordpad

Figure 6.12 Advice on using information resources at Ripon Grammar School, North Yorkshire, UK

reading, note-taking and writing/presenting. These are transferable skills which can be taught to students in the upper primary/elementary and lower secondary/high school and then reinforced within assignment guidelines produced by teachers and school librarians. The following examples show how different elements of the Use part of the PLUS model can be demonstrated to students.

Figure 6.12 shows advice to students at Ripon Grammar School on effective use of information resources, including skimming and scanning.

Once students have located information (e.g. in print or graphic form) on a website, they will take notes on what they have found. Note-taking is a skill that teachers often assume is taught by 'someone else'. For example, in this author's research work, it was found that many secondary/high school teachers often assume that students will bring note-taking skills from primary/elementary school. When primary school teachers were asked about note-taking, many insisted that this was a skill developed at secondary level. Even if stu-

<u>Using Information</u>: Having used the **keywords** to find useful information on your selected websites, now use the writing frame to make notes on the rite of passage which you are researching. Remember the notes must be written in your own words.

Name of Religion:	Name of rite of passage at death:	Sources of information
When does the ceremony to mark the rite of passage take place?		Location: List all the sources of information you have used for this section – following the format of the example used below
What happens in the place of worship (religious building)? Why?		Website author Website title URL
Does anything happen in the home? Why?		
Is there any special food that is eaten? Why?		
Are any special clothes worn? Why?		
Why is this ceremony important for people of this faith?		
Do different groups within this religion conduct this ceremony in different ways? – if so, how and why?		

Figure 6.13   Note-taking at Jack Hunt School, Cambridgeshire, UK

dents have had *some* training in note-taking at primary/elementary level, it is still worthwhile for secondary/high school teachers and school librarians to refresh students' skills in this area. In the PLUS model, students will take notes in relation to Purpose in that they will use the keywords or phrases they identified from brainstorming and concept mapping when taking notes. Figure 6.13 shows an example of scaffolding in the form of a writing frame for students at Jack Hunt School who are doing a Religious Education assignment.

In the PLUS model, as in other models and guidelines, the Use element is a

WORK WITH INFORMATION 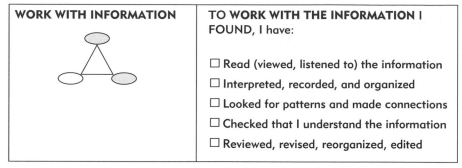	TO WORK WITH THE INFORMATION I FOUND, I have: ☐ Read (viewed, listened to) the information ☐ Interpreted, recorded, and organized ☐ Looked for patterns and made connections ☐ Checked that I understand the information ☐ Reviewed, revised, reorganized, edited

Figure 6.14 Advice on using information at Gladstone Secondary School, Canada (http://gladstone.vsb.bc.ca/library/infolit/RESQUEST%20checklist.doc)

complex mixture of skills and this is summed up in the checklist provided to students at Gladstone Secondary School, shown in Figure 6.14.

The final part of the Use aspect of the PLUS model relates to how students organize their notes and material into a suitable form of presentation, and this will depend on the outcome of the assignment, e.g. a report, an essay or a PowerPoint presentation. At Ripon Grammar School, students are asked to do this in two stages. The first stage is shown in Figure 6.15; it sets students questions that they should ask themselves before starting to write their assignment.

The second stage relates to how students will ensure, first, that their assignment is written in a logical and fluent manner and, second, that they will use the information they have found from print and electronic sources effectively. This advice is shown in Figure 6.16.

The Use stage of the PLUS model allows students to benefit from the

Writing your assignment – part one

When you have finished collecting information, look back at your original planning work.

- Have you answered all the questions you set yourself?
- Do you have enough information from books or the Web to complete your project?
- Are there any gaps in your information? If so, how could you get help in finding what you need?
- Do you think you are ready to write up your work? If not what do you still need to complete?

Figure 6.15 Advice on preparing to write an assignment from Ripon Grammar School, North Yorkshire, UK

Writing your assignment – part two

When you think you are ready to write up your work, you will need to plan how to present your work.

In my introduction I will begin my work with

The main body of my text will include the following main points in this order (you may have fewer than five or you may need to add more)

1.

2.

3.

4.

5.

I will illustrate my work with

I will conclude my work with

Don't forget to include a bibliography listing the print and electronic resources you used for your research!

Figure 6.16 Advice on writing an assignment from Ripon Grammar School, North Yorkshire, UK

Purpose and Location stages because when taking notes and organizing the written or oral presentation, they can use the keywords and ideas found at the earlier stages. A well organized and well written essay or report will be one in which the teacher and school librarian can see evidence of students using critical thinking in finding, evaluating and organizing information and ideas.

On the other hand, a student whose purpose is vague, whose search terms are general and whose evaluation of web material is poor, is unlikely to be able to meet the requirements of a well researched, well organized and well written assignment.

Self-evaluation

The final stage of the PLUS model allows students to reflect on their own work in terms of their output (e.g. a written report or an oral presentation) as well as on the processes which they went through when researching their assignment. As was seen in Chapter 5, even the youngest secondary/high school students are very capable of reflecting on their work and on the PLUS model itself. A recent study by Smith (2003) shows that primary 5 (9-year-old) students in a Scottish school were able to make perceptive comments on their information skills and on the PLUS model. Self-evaluation can help students to focus on how they might improve their work, while analysis of the self-evaluation can help the teacher and school librarian to identify where individual students may need most help.

Students at Ripon Grammar School are required to fill in a self-evaluation sheet as shown in Figure 6.17. The form is seen in the school as representing feedback from the student to the teacher and school librarian but is also viewed as feedback from the students to themselves, which they can reflect on and learn from.

SELF EVALUATING YOUR WORK
After you have finished your project, it is useful to think back over what you have done. This is important as it will help you to improve your research skills!

- What have you enjoyed most about this project?

- What new skills have you learned from doing the PLUS method of research?

- What problems did you have doing your research?

- What would you do differently next time?

- What are you really pleased with? What didn't go exactly as you had planned?

Figure 6.17 Self-evaluation at Ripon Grammar School, North Yorkshire, UK

Self-evaluation – this is checking your work
- Have you answered the question?
- What have you left out?
- What have you done really well?
- What will you do differently in your next project?

Before your Travel Guide is marked:	
1. What have you enjoyed doing in this project?	
2. What has been hard for you to do?	
What do you think about your finished Travel Guide?	
3. It is really good because...	
4. I think my guide would have been better if I...	
After your Travel Guide is marked:	
I have learnt that I can get better marks if I...	

Figure 6.18   Self-evaluation guidance for students at St Ivo School, Cambridgeshire, UK

In St Ivo School, the self-evaluation part of the PLUS model is incorporated into the work which students must submit as part of their project. Figure 6.18 shows guidance on self-evaluation as part of a Religious Education project relating to pilgrims visiting Mecca.

A similar approach to the PLUS model's self-evaluation is taken by Redwood High School, which poses questions to students as shown in Figure 6.19.

Self-evaluation can be seen as the final step in the PLUS model (and in other models) but it can also be seen as the first step towards the student's next assignment because the student should be able to learn from their own self-evaluation and from the teacher's feedback about how to improve elements of their information skills, such as identifying purpose or writing an assignment.

In-service training

One positive way of extending the use of a support structure for students such as the PLUS model in schools is via in-service training sessions where teachers and school librarians can explore issues relating to making their students better

VII. Evaluate the product and process

How well did the project fulfil the assignment and deal with the research topic?

Were the research steps taken appropriate and effective?

By assessing the learning experience, you can identify areas of progress and needs for further improvement. Your teacher may provide a <u>rubric</u> to guide your assessment. Some general issues include:

Did the project meet the need for information and satisfy the task?
Could the research process be expanded or modified?
What new skills and knowledge were gained?
What steps in the research process need further development and practice?

Figure 6.19   Self-evaluation at Redwood High School, CA, USA
(rhsweb.org/library/researchguidelong.htm#Evaluate the product and
process)

assignment planners, better web searchers, better website readers and evaluators, better note-takers and assignment writers/presenters, and better self-evaluators. Different school subjects will stress different aspects of information skills but many skills are relevant across the curriculum. Teachers and school librarians can learn from their fellow professionals in other schools and this learning can then be used as the basis for analysis of information skills and web use in a particular school. Figure 6.20 provides an example of an in-service session designed by the author for use with teachers and school librarians.

Conclusion

The PLUS model is one of a number of information literacy models which have been used in schools to provide students with support or scaffolding when doing assignments. When students are using the web in addition to print and other electronic sources of information, it is even more important for them to be precise in their searching because of the possibility of being presented with a vast range of websites which may be only tangentially relevant to the student's information needs. Teachers and school librarians in the schools that use the PLUS model, as seen in the examples in this chapter, believe that students benefit from all stages in the PLUS model when using the web, as the students not

---

Information skills programmes and the Web

Seminar for teachers and school librarians

Aims
- To examine the key skills needed by secondary school students to use the Web effectively
- To examine ways of integrating the use of websites by students into a school's information skills programme

Methodology
1. Look at the following sites and note down the content of their information skills programmes:
   - www.nudgee.com/library/ – click on **Student guide to preparing and writing assignments**
   - www.mhs.vic.edu.au/home/library – click on **Research**
   - Read the attached pages outlining the PLUS model, the 'Big 6' model and Kuhlthau's research.
2. Participants should split into groups of four or five.
3. Each group should identify what skills students need when using the web, in terms of:
   - The **purpose** for which the student is using the web
   - How students **locate** information on the web
   - How students **use** the information they find on the web
   - How students reflect on their web use via **self-evaluation**.
4. There will now be a discussion on the skills students need to use the web effectively.
5. Each group will be allocated **one** element of the PLUS model and should prepare a lesson plan for teaching that element to students in the first year of the school. The lesson plan (use the attached lesson plan outline) should be related to an actual assignment done in the school, e.g. 'the causes and effects of earthquakes' in Geography.
6. Each group will pass its lesson plan to the next group, until all groups have seen all the lesson plans.
7. There will be a discussion on how to incorporate such lesson plans into the school's information skills programme.

Figure 6.20 In-service session on information skills and the web

only become more sophisticated web searchers but also become more accustomed to critical thinking when planning searches, evaluating website material, selecting and rejecting information, in note-taking, and writing/presenting. Students' ability to be effective self-evaluators means that they can reflect on transferable skills in subsequent assignments. However, while the most able students will, by themselves, constantly improve their skills via reflection, the majority will need reinforcement of their skills via assignments within different subjects. It obviously should not be assumed that students who have used the PLUS model in one assignment will *necessarily* put the relevant skills into practice in another. If the school and school library websites are developed to include a checklist for students who use the PLUS or other models, then students have a *constant* reference point that they can access: a link to this checklist should be included in *all* assignment briefs, whether in printed or electronic form.

References

Barrett, L. and Danks, M. (2003) Information Literacy: a crucial role for schools, *Library & Information Update*, 2 (5) May, 42–4.

Conlon, T. (2002) Information Mapping as a Support for Learning and Teaching, *Computer Education*, (102) (November), 2–12.

McKenzie, J. (2000) *Beyond Technology: questioning, research and the information literate school*, Bellingham, WA, FNO Press.

Smith, K. (2003) *The Primary School Curriculum PLUS Information Skills Models*, unpublished MSc dissertation, Edinburgh, Queen Margaret University College.

Todd, R. (2003) *Learning in the Information Age School: opportunities, outcomes and options*, Keynote Paper, International Association of School Librarianship (IASL) 2003 Annual Conference, Durban, South Africa, 7–11 July 2003, www.iasl-org/conference2003-virtual.html.

7

Developing a school website

. . . .

Having read this chapter, you will be able to:

- identify a clear purpose for your school website
- design a storyboard for your school website
- incorporate key elements of design into your school website
- learn from other schools' sites about how to present information skills guidelines on your school site, particularly in the school library section
- examine the potential for developing a school intranet
- develop in-service training sessions for developing web pages.

. . . .

Introduction

School websites are now recognized as an integral part of a school's information system. However, the *existence* of a school website does not necessarily mean that a school will gain educational value from it. Some school websites appear to exist only because the school is following fashion and copying other schools, or because the website is seen mainly as a marketing tool, with its main audience being *outside* the school. This author would argue that a school website should exist primarily for the benefit of the students and staff in the school and then for the benefit of external users, such as parents and potential students. This is to argue that the site should be driven by the school curriculum and should not be merely a collection of photographs of the school buildings. A school website can be a powerful tool in providing access to learning resources (both print and electronic) for students, staff, parents and other schools. But in order to use these resources effectively, students will need the range of information skills outlined in Chapter 5. Thus *combining* learning resources with guidance on information skills on the school website enhances its value as a learning tool.

The challenge for teachers and school librarians is to design a site that is not simply attractive to students, staff and external users but which is *mainly* a key source of information that supports the school curriculum and has the potential to enhance student learning. This chapter will focus on the development of a school website in relation to:

- the purpose of the site
- the planning and design of the site
- how learning resources and information skills guidance can be incorporated into the site, particularly in its school library section
- how an intranet may be developed
- how in-service sessions can be used to improve contributions to the site from all staff.

Purpose of the site

Developing a website is often referred to as being similar to the development of a building, and the term 'information architecture' is used in website design. However, the development of a school website can be seen more usefully as similar to the information skills process. The PLUS model may be adapted as a guide to website design, as follows:

- Purpose – what is the website for? What is it trying to achieve? Who are the audiences?
- Location – where will the school find the staff and/or students with the skills to design the site? Where will the design team find the resources that will form the site's content?
- Use – how will the site be used? Will it be accessible to its different audiences in terms of language level and reading ability? Will students' learning be improved by using it? Will it have a logical structure which is easily followed?
- Self-evaluation – how will the site be evaluated and monitored so that it remains up to date and innovative? Who will evaluate it?

In relation to purpose, Bellingham Public Schools (2003) state that:

A good home page would do at least three things:

1) Point internal users to good outside information resources
2) Point external and internal visitors to good internal curriculum resources
3) Introduce external visitors to the school.

They argue that library media specialists (school librarians) should 'have a major voice' in the school website's design and development, as they are information professionals whose background and key skills are in information management and retrieval.

Becta (2002) gives the following advice to teachers and school librarians designing school websites:

Ask yourself:

- What is it that I want to 'say' using the web?
- Who will my audience be?
- Why do I feel it is appropriate to use the web for this purpose?
- Are there more effective means of transmitting the information?
- What resources have I got available to me?

The purpose of the school website should be apparent to its users when they access it. For example, Figure 7.1 shows the home page of Wood Green School in the UK. It is clear that the purpose of this site is to provide information to school staff and students and to parents.

Designing a storyboard

One of the most common causes of poor website design is lack of thought about the structure of the site. If a school site is to be visually attractive but also direct users quickly to the information they need, e.g. the school library pages or the homework pages, then the designers will have to work out in advance how this will be done. Storyboarding is a technique which requires teachers and school librarians to put their outline site design on paper. The value of this is that designers can think clearly about structure before designing the actual pages. Fryer (2003) provides an example of storyboarding which can be seen in Figure 7.2 (page 118).

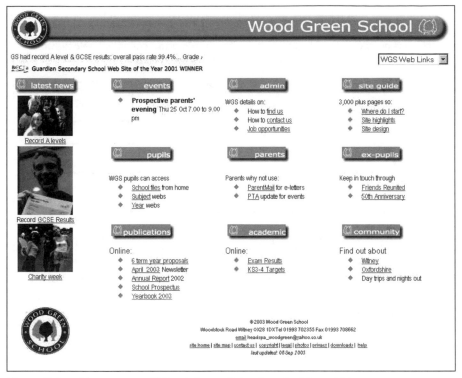

Figure 7.1   Home page of Wood Green School, Oxfordshire, UK
(http://test.woodgreen.oxon.sch.uk)

Another method of storyboarding is for the design team to write down on sticky notes the elements they wish to have on their website, and attach them to a large sheet of paper, so that the elements can be moved easily during discussions about where they can be placed.

Getting the right structure for the school website is the first step towards a logically organized and useable site, so getting the structure of the home page right is crucial. McKenzie (2003) restates a well known phrase in relation to web design:

Tenet Number One: *Less is more*. Take a minimalist approach to page design. Employ few graphics except where the visual contributes meaning ... A menu page should be logically constructed with well ordered lists of choices sufficiently annotated to inform the user of 'what they are getting into'.

- Create separate folders for each section, inside your main folder.
- Put webpages for sections inside their respective folders.
- Here is an example of a storyboard with a main page called 'wheelock.html'. Each section of the website is contained in its own folder.

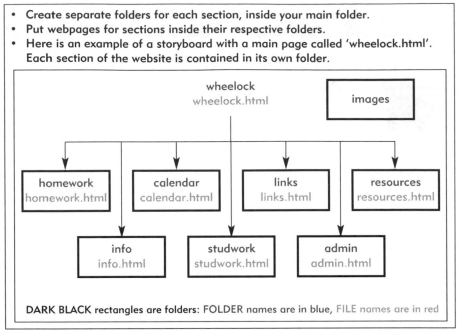

Figure 7.2 Example of storyboarding from www.wtvi.com/html/handout.html

When creating the storyboard for the school website, teachers and school librarians should take this good advice and not be tempted to overcrowd the home page, which gives the user a bewildering range of options. The storyboard should be judged by the simplicity of its design, as seen in Figure 7.2, where the distinct elements of the school site can be clearly seen. Figure 7.3 shows Westminster School's home page, which won a Becta award in the UK. Its effectiveness can be judged by the ease with which a viewer of the site can imagine the storyboard: it is clearly divided into three main sections: for prospective parents and pupils; other sites; and applying for entry to Westminster. These sections are then subdivided into subsections, e.g. the library in the 'other sites' section.

Where possible, the website design team in the school should decide on an initial full storyboard for the site. In relation to Figure 7.2 this would mean that there would be a separate storyboard for each of the elements in the home page. For example, the Year Webs folder might be divided as follows:

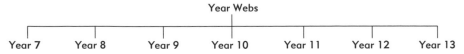

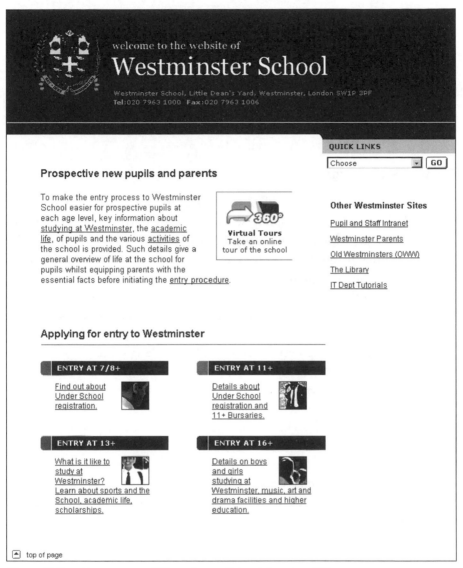

Figure 7.3 Home page of Westminster School, London, UK
(www.westminster.org.uk)

An important factor at this stage is to limit the initial size of the site. The
Web Style Guide (2003) argues that:

One excellent way to keep a tight rein on the overall scope of the site content is to specify a maximum page count in the site specification. Although a page count is hardly infallible as a guide (after all, Web pages can be arbitrarily long), it serves as a constant reminder to everyone involved of the project's intended scope.

A school website should therefore start with a small number of agreed elements and it should not be allowed to grow beyond this size until the design team is satisfied that the site meets the usability standards outlined below.

Elements of design

There are many guidelines available in different countries for teachers and school librarians who are designing school websites. There are some key elements of design which almost all guidelines agree on, but it has to be remembered that design of the website is *not* the first issue that school website design teams should explore. Design has to follow purpose and audience, because users of the website will not be visiting the school website for an aesthetic experience (e.g. to admire original graphics created by students in an art class) but for information or learning experiences.

Becta's (2002) advice on design states that for the design team:

> It is important to consider the design of your web site. The key things to remember are to keep it simple, clear and consistent, and not too heavy in terms of text. Plan your site carefully. Look at other sites to give you an idea of what you do and do not like.

One way to learn from other school websites is to review those that have been included in awards. In the UK, the Becta/*Guardian* UK Education Website Awards (www.becta.org.uk/websiteawards) provide a range of examples from primary/elementary to secondary/high schools; and similar award-winning schools can be seen at Cool School Awards (www.education-world.com/cool_school/#Criteria). For school librarians, the excellent IASL website (www.iasl-slo.org) includes the winners of the IASL/Concorde awards. Figure 7.4 shows an example of part of a very simple but effective school library website home page.

The *Web Style Guide* (2003), McKenzie (2003) and Becta (2002) all suggest that the following elements of design need careful consideration:

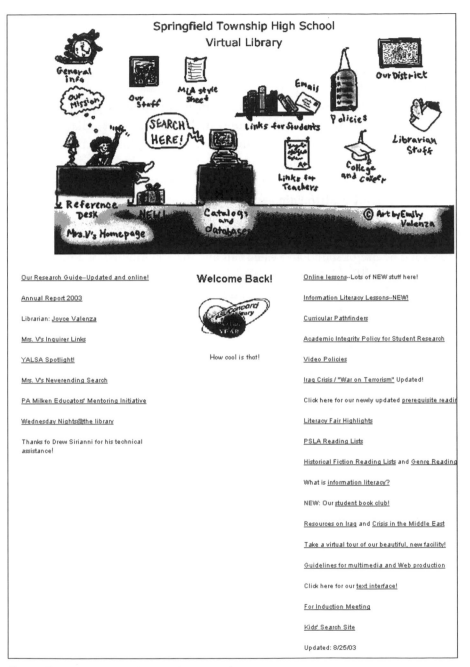

Figure 7.4   Example of school library web page
(http://mciunix.mciu.k12.pa.us/~spjvweb)

- **Colour** – while the choice of colours may be subjective, designers should avoid colours that are too bright either as text or background. Black text on a pale cream background is a safe option to begin with. Colour should be used to ease reading and identification of links but *not* as an attempt to impress the website user.
- **Format** – the design format should be consistent throughout the site so that the user can move smoothly around it. McKenzie notes that 'Speed of movement is enhanced by repeating basic formats', and Becta argues that 'consistent placing of elements and navigation buttons not only saves time but also helps people with special needs to use the site'.
- **Graphics and multimedia** – while graphics can enhance the look and usability of a site and are particularly useful for students using the school website, they should be clearly labelled and should not take a long time to load. The use of sound and video can enhance the quality of a school website but may also be seen as unnecessary distractions.
- **Navigation** – even the most inexperienced user of the site should be able to move smoothly around it. Each page should have a consistent link back to the home page and there should be a site map to aid users. Where possible, a search facility should be included, especially on large sites. No user should have to use more than three mouse-clicks to get where they want to be on the site.
- **Links** – access to resources on a school website will be an essential element, particularly on the library web pages and on subject web pages. Links should be clearly marked and should be to a specific part of another website. McKenzie argues that 'When linking to other WWW locations, strip away time-wasting top levels of those sites, provide addresses which take users directly to good information and include thorough annotations explaining what can be found at those locations.' Regular checking is necessary to make links work. Software such as Xenu's Link Sleuth (http://home.snafu.de/tilman/xenulink.html) can be used to check links.
- **Information for users** – users of the site should be consistently made aware of when the site was last updated, who owns the copyright and whom to contact on matters relating to the site (include 'snail-mail' as well as e-mail addresses and a telephone/fax number). Each page should have a clear title so that users know where they are on the site.
- **Accessibility** – the site should be accessible to *all* potential users. Becta states that 'One in five people has special needs of one sort or another' and that

school sites should try to meet guidelines set out in relevant disability legislation. Becta also suggests that 'For further advice on designing your web pages with accessibility in mind, including navigation, using frames, scrolling text, plug-ins, JavaScript and Shockwave, go to the Royal National Institute for the Blind's Accessible Web Design page (www.rnib.org.uk/digital/hints.htm).' The use of software such as Flash or Shockwave should be carefully considered when planning alternatives for disabled users.

- **Tools** – there is a range of tools that can be used to create web pages, some of which are free on the web. More sophisticated tools such as Dreamweaver (www.macromedia.com/software/dreamweaver) or FrontPage (www.microsoft.com/frontpage) can be used to create more complex school websites, as they provide a variety of short-cuts to creating links and including multimedia. Most guidelines advise that at least one member of a web design team should have knowledge of HTML (Hypertext Mark Up Language) because this forms the basic code of most websites; when problems arise, a solution may lie in altering the code. Inexperienced teachers and school librarians wishing to learn HTML can use sources such as HTML Tutorial (www.w3schools.com/tutorial). Web pages can also be created using packages such as Microsoft® Word™ but care must be taken: such packages often use unnecessary HTML or include code that is not recognizable by browsers such as Netscape Navigator.

The above design elements should be seen as essential and interlinked elements in good web design for schools. It is the *combination* of good design elements which will make a school website easily accessible, readable and navigable.

Information skills on the school website

One of the purposes of an effective school website should be to provide students with access to learning resources, and this can be done directly by providing links to online resources via specific URLs or gateways or subscription services such as Newsbank. The website should also provide indirect access to important resources, such as books and reports in print form and CD-ROMs, by providing either a link to the library catalogue via the website or information about the location of books and CD-ROMs. A school website can also encourage the reading of fiction by including student book reviews and links to authors' websites. If students are going to be effective learners by using print and electronic resources, they will need the information skills outlined in Chapter 5. The school website can be an excellent vehicle for providing students with online guidelines to such learning skills.

However, to be an effective vehicle for presenting information skills guidelines to students, the school website should not merely contain a list of skills or a list of links to websites on how to use a search engine. There should be some interactivity in the presentation of information skills guidelines and students should be able to put their skills into practice when using different formats. There is an unfortunate tendency for some school websites (usually in the school library section) to concentrate merely on information skills related to using web-based resources. This will tend to reinforce student views that 'everything is on the web' and that skills such as using a search engine are in some way superior to skills such as identifying purpose or note-taking. The following examples show how a school website can be a vehicle that students can use both to learn about information skills *and* to apply the skills.

Under the title *Student Guides*, St Joseph's Nudgee College Library in Australia (www.nudgee.com/library) provides students with an online guide to information skills, covering the use of print and electronic learning resources. Figure 7.5 shows part of the *Student Guides* page.

If a student clicks on 'How do I plan and write an assignment', they are presented with six stages. as shown in Figure 7.6.

If the student scrolls down to Stage 1 – Plan – one skill that is explained is how to define the purpose of the assignment, as shown in Figure 7.7.

There is a comprehensive and easy-to-follow guide to the whole range of information skills provided by this site, which means that it can be used by teachers and librarians working with students but also by students independently.

Another example of a well presented and applicable information skills guideline is presented on the Melbourne High School Library web pages (www.mhs.vic.edu.au). This is a comprehensive guide to information skills and contains a model for students to use and practical examples that can be used either by teachers and teacher–librarians with students or by students on their own. Figure 7.8 shows part of the information skills guidelines in which the school provides students with a checklist that they can fill in when they are doing an assignment. This is useful to the students, as they can monitor their own progress, but also to the teachers and teacher–librarians in the school who can check on student progress.

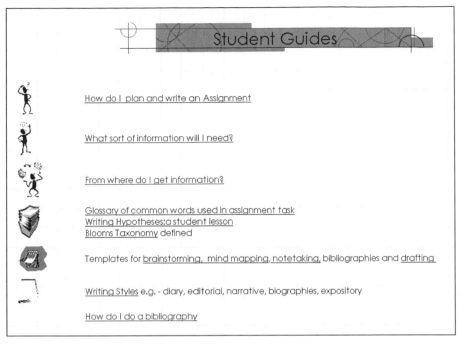

Figure 7.5 Part of the Student Guides page at St Joseph's Nudgee College, Australia (www.nudgee.com/library/)

Stage 1	Stage 2	Stage 3	Stage 4	Stage 5	Stage 6
Plan	Prepare	Action	Synthesize	Present	Evaluate

Figure 7.6 The six stages of information skills at St Joseph's College, Australia (www.nudgee.com/library/)

Step 1. Deconstruct/Define

To make sense of a question we have to deconstruct it. This is how you do it -

- Read your task and then underline or highlight the main words.
- Try to work out the meanings of these words.
- Use a dictionary if you have to.
- You will often find the meanings of words in the glossary of your text book.

Figure 7.7 Defining purpose at St Joseph's College, Australia (www.nudgee.com/library/)

A Research Process Checklist

Name   **Form**

Deciding
* My task is to . .
* Some key words and ideas related to my task are . .

Finding
* I expect to find information by using . .

Using
* For this project I have already used the following resources successfully . .

Evaluating – return to – **Deciding**
* I need to get more information about . .

Finding (some more)
* I expect to get this information from . .

 DON'T FORGET – think about how you managed your research – is there a better way to do it?

Figure 7.8   The Research Process Checklist from Melbourne High School, Australia (www.mhs.vic.edu.au/home/library/infoproc/chres.doc)

Teachers and school librarians wishing to display the school's information skills guidelines for students can benefit from studying such examples as those from St Joseph's Nudgee College and Melbourne High School, and thinking about how their own school's advice on information skills might be presented. It must be remembered that if a school wishes to use some of the web pages presented from the two Australian schools, permission must be obtained as copyright will apply.

Developing an intranet

Many schools in different parts of the world are now developing intranets in order to exploit further the possibilities of ICT in the school. An intranet will contain a range of information for staff, students and sometimes parents. Users of the intranet access that information using internet technology, so a school

Figure 7.9 Home page of Cramlington Community High School, Norhumbria, UK (www.cchs.northumbria.sch.uk)

intranet will be accessed using a browser such as Internet Explorer. However, the difference between using the school website and using the intranet is that a user will have to be a recognized member of the school community and will need to have a user name and password which allows them to log on to the school intranet. A key security aspect of an intranet is that it protects school information from access by general internet users. Figure 7.9 shows the home page of Cramlington Community High School, which is accessible by anyone using the internet. However, members of the school community have access to

Cramlington Community High School					
HOME	INTRANET	SUBJECTS	SEARCH	LRC	STAFF
About Us	Who we are, where we are, contact details...				
The Intranet	Our students use the Intranet to access over 85, 000 files of educational resources in school. Every department has its own web site and is developing interactive on-line resources to enhance students' learning. Note: not everything is uploaded onto our Internet site				
Accelerated Learning	Our school has been involved in Accelerated Learning since 1997 after an inspirational visit from Alistair Smith. This section explains more and includes downloadable resources.				
Parents	Find out about our Ofsted report, school holidays, our 'home school' agreement etc.				

Figure 7.10 Intranet home page at Cramlington Community High School, Northumbria, UK (www.cchs.northumbria.sch.uk)

the school intranet, part of which is displayed in Figure 7.10.

The key areas covered by school intranets tend to be:

- learning and teaching materials such as lesson plans, instructional websites, resource guides
- online access to the school library catalogue
- student information such as timetables, details of school events and school sports
- staff information such as timetables, school notices, curriculum syllabi, school events
- administrative information for staff only, such as student files, exam results, confidential school reports, committee minutes.

Carter's (2002) research on the development of intranets and the role of the school librarian in Scottish secondary schools found that while educational authorities had a limited view of the development of intranets, some individual schools were more focused on the use of the intranet as a learning and teaching tool. Carter identifies a number of roles that school librarians, working collaboratively with teachers, have undertaken. These are:

- intranet builder – designing and implementing the school intranet from scratch
- intranet manager – gathering and uploading information for the intranet and editing the intranet content
- intranet mediator – identifying online resources to support intranet content such as instructional websites or, in one school, 'Homework Support Pages'
- content creators – creating materials for the intranet such as instructional websites and information skills guides.

In schools such as Linlithgow Academy (see examples in Chapter 8), which have established intranets, the development of the intranet has been the result of a combination of skills from school professionals including the ICT co-ordinator, the school librarian, computing staff and individual teachers. The development of school intranets is still at an early stage in many schools but it is clear that many others also wish to secure access to their learning and teaching materials so that students can benefit from this security. This does not mean that schools will not retain school websites that contain *some* of the material available on the intranet. The potential of a school intranet is enormous, particularly in providing student access to instructional websites, learning support such as information skills guidelines, and access to online information resources. The key to successful intranet development is collaboration between school management, ICT co-ordinators, teachers and school librarians.

In-service training

Developing a school website should be a collective activity, so in-service training sessions attended both by teachers and by the school librarian will be the most profitable means of ensuring that the school has the site that it wants and that reflects the culture of the school. Those involved in designing in-service training for teachers and school librarians should be careful not to fall into the 'technology trap': designing sessions that concentrate solely on using software such as Dreamweaver to design web pages. While this is a necessary part of in-service training, it is clear from what has been discussed above in this chapter that website design and development are as much about purpose and content as they are about design. An example of an in-service session designed by this author (Figure 7.11) shows the need for careful thought about purpose and content. This session is accompanied by a website development workshop in which teachers and school librarians are given an opportunity to create some web pages using Dreamweaver software.

Conclusion

School websites are now seen as essential tools for promoting learning and teaching, enhancing communication with parents and providing external links for students to use. School librarians have been at the forefront of web design in many schools and their role as information professionals should not be underestimated by school web design teams. If school websites are to be effective in contributing to the improvement of learning in the school, the provision of access to print and online resources will be required. However, these resources will be exploited to their full extent only if the students are equipped with the necessary range of information skills; providing online guidelines for students to define purpose, locate and use resources, and evaluate their own skills should be an item high on the list of potential school website content.

Developing the school website and promoting use

Seminar for teachers and school librarians

Aims
- to evaluate the style and content of selected school websites
- to identify the purpose and potential content of school websites
- to discuss ways in which teachers and school librarians can effectively promote the school website.

Methodology

Evaluating style and content
Go to the following sites in turn and write notes on how effective each website is in relation to:
- purpose – what is this website trying to achieve?
- style – layout and use of logos, graphics and colours
- navigation – following links from the home page
- content – is the content clear and suitable?

Websites
1. Royal Grammar School, High Wycombe, Buckinghamshire, UK (www.rgshw.com)
2. Hampstead School, London, UK (www.hampsteadschool.org.uk)
3. Hinchingbrooke School, Cambridgeshire, UK (www.hinchbk.cambs.sch.uk)

Purpose and content
- participants will split into groups of four or five
- each group will discuss the **purpose** of having a school website and identify **two** key benefits of having a school website
- each group will discuss the content of a school website and identify **four** elements that **must** be included in all school websites.

Promotion
Each group will discuss the promotion of the website by examining:

a) who will use the school website? and
b) how will the website be promoted in the school and externally? and
c) how can the school website be a vehicle for increasing use of the school's print and electronic resources?

The group should make **two** key points in relation to a), b) and c).
There will a plenary discussion of the points with each group being asked to explain their conclusions.

Figure 7.11 In-service session on developing a school website

Schools developing intranets can produce secure learning environments for students and expand online learning and access to resources in the school.

References

Becta (2002) *Designing Effective Websites*, www.becta.org.uk.

Bellingham Public Schools (2003) *Designing School Homepages*, www.bham.wednet.edu/technology/webrules.htm.

Carter, M. (2002) The Connecting School and the Intranet Librarian, *School Libraries Worldwide*, **8** (2) (July), 51–64.

Fryer, A. (2003) *Writing Webpages with Wesley*, www.wtvi.com/html/handout.html.

McKenzie, J. (2003) *Home Sweet Home: creating WWW pages that deliver*, http://fno.org.

Web Style Guide (2003) www.webstyleguide.com.

8

Developing an instructional website

Having read this chapter, you will be able to:

- identify effective approaches to instructional website design
- evaluate a range of instructional websites in schools in different countries
- apply techniques in designing an instructional website
- design an instructional website which encourages the use of a wide range of resources and includes advice on information skills in your instructional website
- learn from a case study of collaboration between teachers and the school librarian
- develop instructional websites using Filamentality and WebQuests.

Introduction

Instructional websites are now becoming common in secondary/high schools in different countries as teachers and school librarians realize the potential advantages of giving students access to online learning materials. The availability of new authoring tools such as Dreamweaver (www.macromedia.com/software/dreamweaver) and FrontPage (www.microsoft.com/frontpage) means that designing a website is now a much simpler task for teachers and school librarians as they do not need to have sophisticated programming knowledge. There is a wide variety of instructional websites on the internet and on school intranets as well as a range of definitions of what constitutes an instructional website. This author would define instructional websites as websites which:

- are designed by individuals or groups of school staff
- are related to the curriculum
- contain information from which students can learn
- engage students in critical thinking by posing questions
- contain links to print and/or electronic resources for students to use
- encourage students to use information skills
- include, where appropriate, multimedia features such as graphics, photographs, sound and video.

The examples cited in this chapter range from the simple to the sophisticated in terms of design but the *purpose* of the instructional website is paramount and an easily constructed WebQuest may be more appropriate in some cases than a complex site. This chapter will focus on:

- effective approaches to instructional website design
- criteria for the evaluation of instructional websites
- techniques used to develop an instructional website
- the inclusion of resources and information skills guidance in an instructional website
- a case study of instructional websites collaboratively designed by teachers and a school librarian
- the use of Filamentality and WebQuests to develop instructional websites.

Approaches to instructional website design – purpose and audience

Instructional website design is in many ways similar to the design of a school website seen in Chapter 7, in that there has to be a clear purpose, the contents have to be relevant, the site has to be useable and easily navigated, the use of colour and multimedia has to be appropriate and the site has to be kept up to date. However, instructional websites are designed for use by students at different levels in the school so their audience is clearly different. Whereas a school website seeks to provide information for a wide market – school management, teachers, school librarians, other school staff, students, parents, other schools and the general public – an instructional website serves a niche market and is aimed at students with particular needs. Thus, in designing an instructional website, teachers and school librarians have to focus on the *purpose* of the website – to meet the needs of a particular part of the school curriculum – and the *audience*, i.e. the students (and possibly their parents).

Community High School District 99's (2003) guidelines on designing what are termed 'Teacher Web Sites' state that the purpose of an instructional website is to:

- List assignments
- Showcase student work
- Access grades
- Link to subject references
- Provide information to parents
- List contact information:
    Email address
    Phone number
    Office hours
- Announce dates of field trips and permission forms
- Produce online activities such as WebQuests
- Provide online forms for electronic student response.

Bafile (2002) quotes a physics teacher's purpose in creating an instructional website: 'I created *St. Mary's Physics Online* to better serve the educational needs of my eleventh grade students. ... My goal was to make everything on the Web site very practical. I wanted it to be useful, highly organized, and to load quickly.'

Moore (2001) provides advice for history teachers and argues that 'We should have real-world subject knowledge, and understanding of how to communicate this to particular audiences [in order] to create a resource or collection of resources with a clear subject focus and sensitivity to the potential audience.' McKenzie (2002) adds that another purpose of an instructional website is to provide students with scaffolding when completing an assignment, and this includes: 'clear directions, clarity of purpose, pointers to resources, clear expectations, assessment rubrics, efficiency, momentum and on task behaviour'.

Teachers and school librarians teaching information skills rightly emphasize the importance of purpose and audience to their students; and they, in turn, need a clear purpose and a clear identification of audience(s) if they are to design websites that become part of their students' learning experience.

Evaluating instructional websites

McKenzie (2002) states that at the third stage of 'Building research modules' (i.e. instructional websites that include an emphasis on the information skills process for students) 'the team moves on to visit and consider the attributes of projects built by teachers from schools around the world. By evaluating the work of others, the team begins to develop a personal definition of an effective research module.'

Teachers and school librarians involved in designing instructional websites can examine a range of websites available on the web and can focus on sites relating to their particular subject. Once suitable sites have been identified, teachers and school librarians can use some of the criteria for evaluating websites identified in Chapter 3 but need to remember that the purposes of instructional websites differ from those of websites designed for students to find information. In evaluating instructional websites, the criteria to be used should include:

- Purpose – is it clear what the site is trying to accomplish?
- Level – is it clear for which level/grade of student the site is designed?
- Language – is the level of language appropriate to the students who will use the site?
- Content – is the content of the website clearly outlined in the home page and is the content appropriate for that subject and those students?
- Structure – is the site well organized and logically structured, e.g. in guiding students to external links or explaining the assessment aspect to them?
- Design – is the website attractive to students in its use of colour, graphics and multimedia?
- Differentiation – does the site make allowances for students of different abilities studying the same subject? Are alternative sources suggested?
- Information skills – does the site provide students with guidance (direct or indirect) on purpose, location, use and self-evaluation?
- Adaptation – could this site be adapted (with permission) for use in my school for my particular need, e.g. year 7 (11-year-old) geography students studying the causes of earthquakes?

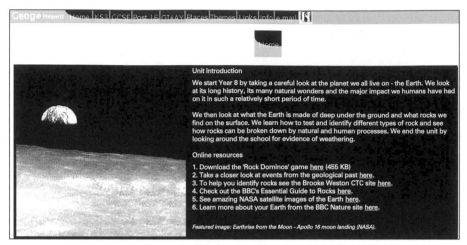

Figure 8.1   Part of instructional website for the Hewett School, Norfolk, UK
(www.hewett.norfolk.sch.uk/curric/NEWGEOG/Index.htm)

It is unlikely that any instructional website reviewed will meet all of the criteria above, so teachers and school librarians will have to decide which criteria are most important for their own purposes. Figure 8.1 shows an example of part of an instructional website for students of the Hewett School, UK. It is a good example of a well designed site, which has a clear purpose and an attractive design.

Design techniques

As with school website design, seen in Chapter 7, there are many guides on the web to designing instructional websites. Some of the best advice can be found from practitioners who have developed their own websites and are self-taught. Gardner (2003) states that the first rule is 'Keep the design simple' and advises teachers and school librarians:

> Use pale or even white backgrounds, which are easy on the eye, this will allow the user to focus on your content. Decide on a particular style and colour scheme and maintain it throughout the site, this will help visitors navigate the site. Creating a house style and using templates also saves time and helps those with special needs use the site.

Bafile (2002) also urges simplicity of design in relation to the users' ability to access the site easily. Although instructional websites may be used mainly in the school, students (and possibly parents) may wish to view the sites from home, and Bafile quotes a school librarian who argues:

> Try to design an attractive but simple site that anyone can use, regardless of modem speed or computer type ... don't assume they all use the most-advanced computers and cable modems. If you put sounds or special effects on the site, set a button so visitors can turn them off.

A second key aspect of design is the website designer's knowledge of the technical aspects of instructional website design. History teacher Moore (2001) argues that teachers and school librarians will need *some* knowledge of HTML as 'Knowing how HTML works is very useful for some things – like making pages display in the way you want them to in different browsers.' Moore states that for many instructional website designers

> More common, and perhaps more popular are HTML editors which have a WYSI-WYG (what you see is what you get) interface – like ... Dreamweaver. These show you more or less how your pages appear in a 'design view'. For most people doing most tasks, most of the time, they will make things easier. But they will also do things you don't quite understand. Some of them may offer to take over the design of your whole site.

Thus, a combination of some HTML knowledge and the ability to use a commercial package such as Dreamweaver (www.macromedia.com/software/dreamweaver) is most useful. Using Dreamweaver at an elementary level is very similar to using a package such as Microsoft® Word™ for Windows and adding graphics and photographs from files is very straightforward. Figure 8.2 shows a simple page created in Dreamweaver.

Figure 8.3 shows the same page viewed in HTML. In Figure 8.3, creating links from the words that appear in blue and underlined on screen is done using icons or the **Modify** menu in Dreamweaver. In HTML, the code

```
<a href="fig9.3.1">skills</a>
```

is used to provide a link with page for skills.

A further key area for teachers and school librarians to focus on when

---

James Herring's PLUS Model
PURPOSE * LOCATION * USE * SELF-EVALUATION

This site aims to provide teachers and school librarians with:

** An outline of the <u>skills</u> which students will learn when using the PLUS model

** <u>Examples</u> of how the PLUS model is used in schools

** <u>Research</u> into the use of the PLUS model at Ripon Grammar School

** <u>Links</u> to other information literacy sites

Figure 8.2   Example of a page created in Dreamweaver
(www.macromedia.com/software/dreamweaver)

designing an instructional website is the careful balance of text and graphics. Moore (2001) advises:

> In designing pages, you should think of a kind of narrative or sequence and structure for documents. What is the function of images in this? Are they crucial to understanding, helpful as interpretation, or merely there as embellishment?

A well designed instructional website is likely to have a home page with both text and graphics, but only a limited amount of text, likely to be in a large font. Subsequent pages may have more text as they may contain a project outline or guidance for students. Figure 8.4 shows a well designed home page for an instructional science website.

When students click on **Interpreting Data**, they are taken to a page that is more text-based, but the use of more text is more appropriate here because of the need for students to get information on guidelines for project completion. Figure 8.5 shows details of the students' task.

In relation to graphics, software packages such as Dreamweaver (www. macromedia.com/software/dreamweaver) can provide reasonably sophisticated graphical elements but for *more* sophisticated graphics manipulation programs, teachers and school librarians should consider buying Adobe Photoshop (www.adobe.com). There are also many free graphics on the web, such as

```
<html>
<head>
<title>Untitled Document</title>
<meta http-equiv="Content-Type" content="text/html;
charset=iso-8859-1">
</head>
<body bgcolor="#FFFFFF" text="#000000">
<div align="center"><font size="6"
color="#000000">James Herring's PLUS
Model</font></div>
<p align="center"><font size="6"
color="#000000">PURPOSE * LOCATION * USE * SELF-
EVALUATION</font></p>
<p><font size="5" color="#000000">This site aims to
provide teachers and school librarians
with:</font></p>
<p> </p>
<p><font size="5" color="#000000">** An outline of the
<a href="fig9.3.1">skills</a> which students will
learn when using the PLUS model</font></p>
<p> </p>
<p><font size="5" color="#000000">**
<a href="fig9.3.2">Examples</a> of how the PLUS model
is used in schools</font></p>
<p> </p>
<p><font size="5" color="#000000">**
<a href="fig9.3.4">Research</a> into the use of the
PLUS model at Ripon Grammar School</font></p>
<p> </p>
<p><font size="5" color="#000000">**
<a href="fig9.3.5">Links</a> to other information
literacy sites</font><font color="#000000"><br>
</font> </p>
</body>
</html>
```

Figure 8.3   Dreamweaver page viewed in HTML

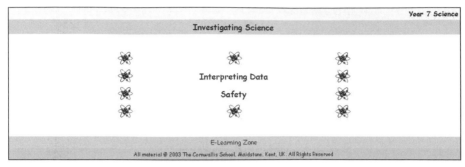

Figure 8.4 Investigating science for year 7 students at Cornwallis School, Kent, UK (www.cornwallis.kent.sch.uk)

Design Gallery Live (http://dgl.microsoft.com) or Classroom Clipart (http://classroomclipart.com). Using graphics can certainly add interest to a site and make it more attractive to students but care must be taken to avoid the use of graphics merely to impress. Graphics should add to the content of the site and not distract the use from that content.

There are many other 'rules' for good instructional website design and these

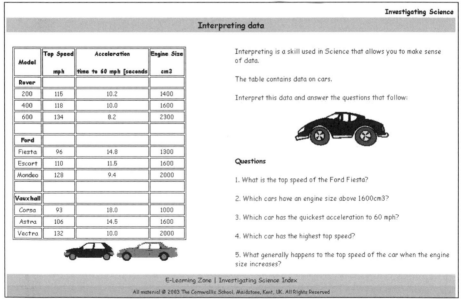

Figure 8.5 Science task for year 7 students at Cornwallis School, Kent, UK (www.cornwallis.kent.sch.uk)

can be summarized as:

- Once the site becomes larger, remember the 'three-click' rule which means that anyone using the site should be able to get from any one point on the site to another using no more than three clicks.
- Providing links to external sites is a key benefit of instructional websites for students, as this allows them to explore sites which have been mediated by the teacher and school librarian. Links should be provided to specific parts of large websites so that students can gain access to relevant information immediately. For example, a link to information on earthquakes in California should be to http://geopubs.wr.usgs.gov/fact-sheet/fs094-96/ and not just to http://earthquake.usgs.gov/ as this is the home page of the US Geological Survey Earthquake Hazard Program.
- Using frames is not advisable as they are difficult to design, may confuse students and limit the site's listing on search engines.
- The site should contain a copyright statement to protect the intellectual content of the site and, where appropriate, a disclaimer stating that the web-site designers believe that all graphics or images used are copyright-free or permission for their use has been granted.
- The site should have an indication of when it was last updated and there should be a contact e-mail address on the site. This is important if the site is to be available on the web as part of the overall school website

Resources and information skills

Instructional websites provide students with a variety of learning features, including:

- information on a topic (e.g. an explanation of the causes of World War 1)
- assignment or activity outlines (e.g. 'Write a 1000-word essay on the effects of famine in a particular country.')
- simple tests (e.g. 'Identify which of the following are primary or secondary historical sources.').

One of the key learning features in an instructional website is the provision of a range of resources for students to use when investigating a topic or completing an assignment. In many cases, the provision of a list of print and electronic resources is more useful to students than advice on using a search engine because a resources list will represent resources that have been specifically selected and evaluated by the teacher and school librarian. Figure 8.6 shows an example of a list of resources provided for students at Hinchingbrooke School doing an assignment on World War 1, and includes part of the page listing online resources and part of the page listing print resources.

Instructional websites often contain elements of information skills that students need to complete an assignment or investigation and this may well be in addition to a more comprehensive guide to information skills provided on the school website – often in the library or media centre pages. This is a very useful reminder to students of the need for them to adapt their information skills, whether Purpose, Location, Use or Self-evaluation, to the needs of a particular assignment. Figure 8.7 (page 144) shows advice given to students doing an essay on *Hamlet* and covers elements of Use including reading for information, note-taking and organizing an essay.

From these examples, it can be seen that teachers and school librarians who design instructional websites can incorporate advice to students not only on *where* to find resources but also on *how* to use these resources effectively. This reinforcement of information skills guidance ensures that students will be made aware of the importance of information skills when researching and writing.

Collaboration between teachers and the school librarian: a case study of Linlithgow Academy

Linlithgow Academy is a secondary comprehensive school in West Lothian, Scotland and is one of the pioneer schools in the UK in terms of developing the use of ICT across the curriculum. The enthusiasm for and knowledge of ICT is shared by school management and school staff. This school is well equipped in terms of student access to computers but not exceptionally so. While other schools of a similar size and status have *more* equipment, what distinguishes Linlithgow Academy is not the number of computers they have but how they are used, along with other learning resources.

There is a well established tradition of collaboration between the school librarian, Chris Morrison, and the teaching staff. This covers team work on information skills with a range of departments, the development of the school intranet, identification and evaluation of print and electronic resources and

The Battlefields

- **A World War I Chronology - What happened and When**
- **Commonwealth War Graves (with searchable index)**
- **Biographies of World War I Poets**
- **Trenches on The Web**
- **Canada in the First World War and the Road to Vimy Ridge**
- **Canadian War Monuments**
- **Canadian Books of Remembrance**
- **Lord Strathcona's Horse, Royal Canadian Regiment**

FURTHER RESEARCH

All the following books are in <u>Hinchingbrooke Resources Centre</u>

The Pictorial History of World War I ~ G D Sheffield

- Battle of The Somme ~ Christopher Martin
- The Airman's War 1914-18 ~ Peter H Liddle
- World War I: 1914 ~ Philip J Haythornthwaite
- An Australian in the First World War ~ Bill Gamage
- A Military Atlas of the First World War ~ Arthur Banks
- An Illustrated Companion to the First World War ~ Anthony Bruce
- Contemporary Accounts of the First World War ~ John Simpkin
- Death's Men : Soldiers of The Great War ~ Denis Winter
- Goodbye To All That ~ Robert Graves
- The Great War ~ Vincent Crinnion
- History of World War I ~ A J P Taylor

You might also read **Birdsong** by Sebastian Faulks and **The Ghost Road** by Pat Barker. These two novels are quite simply **superb** evocations of the time, though the language at times may be more suitable to those over 16.

Figure 8.6   Resource guide for students at Hinchingbrooke School, Cambridgeshire, UK

William Shakespeare's

Hamlet

Student Activity 1: The Main Character

The Task:
Write an essay discussing the character of *Hamlet* in William Shakespeare's Hamlet. In this essay, attempt to explain why Hamlet does not avenge his father's murder immediately upon learning of the murder from the dead king's ghost at the end of Act 1.

The Process:
• Through your study of the play, determine which characteristics of Hamlet would move him toward immediate action and which would cause him to delay action. Consider the weakening effect of the emotional trauma Hamlet experienced prior to the opening scene of the play. Try to imagine the effect such trauma would have on you and your ability to act decisively.

Next, study well the essays given to you as resources. They are attempts to explain the play, some focusing specifically on the question of Hamlet's delay in killing his uncle and king, Claudius. Take notes on what you find in these essays. Finally, using your understanding of Hamlet's characteristics and your notes on the essays you've read, write your composition.
• Begin with a strong thesis statement which identifies Hamlet as the protagonist of William Shakespeare's drama *Hamlet* and which states the opinion that Hamlet's delay in killing his uncle Claudius is understandable;
• Focus on Hamlet's reasons for wanting to kill his uncle Claudius;
• Discuss Hamlet's characteristics citing certain of his characteristics and emotional condition as reasons for his delay in killing Claudius;
• End with a strong closing statement

Figure 8.7   Advice to students studying *Hamlet* from the SCORE Project in California, USA (www.sdcoe.k12.ca.us/score/cla.html)

organizing student use of the library. Recently, this collaboration has taken the form of the joint development of instructional websites with the History, Geography, English, and Religious and Moral Education departments. This case study will focus on how the librarian and a geography teacher, Barbara Lee, co-operated in developing a site entitled 'Earth Forces' and also on how the librarian co-ordinated a website entitled 'Issues' with a range of teachers in the school.

Earth Forces

The origin of the Earth Forces website stemmed from the desire of the geography teacher to produce an online guide to an S2 (second year of secondary/high school) geography class. The teacher was aware that the school librarian had expertise in using Dreamweaver and that he had jointly created an instructional website on New Lanark with a history teacher. This site is part of the school's website and can be found at www.westlothian.org.uk/Linlithgow-Ac/localcommunity/newlanark/index.htm. After discussion with the school librarian on the aims of the Earth Forces website, the teacher used a tutorial designed by the school librarian which included a template for instructional website design. This template is now being used as a template for the whole school and has the advantage of making students familiar with a standard design of instructional websites in different subjects. The site was then uploaded on to the school's intranet and is not yet part of the school website.

The Earth Forces site was created because the teacher felt that although students had access to the web to find materials for their projects relating to earthquakes and volcanoes, they tended to try to use search engines to find materials rather than the bookmarked sites provided. In an interview with the author, the teacher stated:

> We felt that by creating a user friendly resource on the Intranet, which would channel them towards relevant resources on the internet, and also point them in the direction of other printed or electronic resources, the time they spent on the PC would be more productive. Also, it meant that they could access the information and guidance on the project from any room in the school, and at any time, including Homework Club when their class teacher wasn't there.

The teacher, Barbara Lee, identified the advantages of using the Earth Forces site as follows:

- The students were motivated when using the site, especially as the site could be updated throughout the duration of the project.
- The site was easier for students to use than handouts, and more graphics and photographs could be used.
- Students could work more independently and could also work with each other via the bulletin board.

Earth Forces Website

Welcome to the S2 Earth Forces Website!

Dear Geographer,

Welcome to the S2 Earth Forces Website! The Earth Forces unit is absolutely brilliant!

In class you will learn about the enchanting Earth, riveting rocks, pulsing plates, notable natural disasters and magnificent mountain building! You can find out more about these topics by visiting the links on this page. There are <u>classwork</u> links, homework links and links and pages to help you prepare for your test and <u>project</u>. The <u>Bulletin Board</u> will help keep you up to date, and to find out key information on natural disasters, why not visit the <u>Earthquakes</u> and <u>Volcanoes</u> pages?? Enjoy wandering through the site, surfing the net and learning about Geography. If you have ideas about how the site could be improved, please speak to your Geography teacher.

From,

Mr Raeburn, Mrs Easson, Mr Doherty, Miss Russell, and Miss Lee

Last updated: August 2003, by the Geography Department
Every effort has been made to acknowledge the sources of all photographs/diagrams used in this website.
Please advise the Geography department if any additional copyright information can be added.

 Linlithgow Academy Geography Department

Figure 8.8 Earth Forces home page at Linlithgow Academy, Scotland, UK

- The quality of students' work improved, especially that of lower ability students who often had difficulty in identifying relevant materials.
- Students became more comfortable using a range of materials in the library and more easily combined information from books, journals, CD-ROMs and websites. The more able students still used search engines to good effect and thus retained independence.
- Increased co-operation with the school librarian meant that the teacher gained new ICT skills; students now work better in the school library; the school librarian's feedback on student work in the library is useful to the teacher.

Figure 8.8 shows part of the home page of the Earth Forces site. It is a good example of simple yet effective design, making good use of text, graphics and colour. It also presents its content and its aims clearly. In the full home page, buttons for links to the project, bulletin board and classwork are provided.

Within the site, there are details for students about the project which they will undertake and Figure 8.9 shows the information students obtain when clicking on the project link in Figure 8.8.

The site also provides students with information skills advice which is obtained by clicking on the **planning page** link in Figure 8.9. This advice is shown in Figure 8.10.

Issues

The Issues website originated because of increased demand in the curriculum for resources that could be used across a number of subjects and could also be used by a range of different students. The Issues site caters for students in years 2 to 4 in the school and this can mean that up to 200 students are seeking similar information at one time. The school librarian had been bookmarking sites for students in the library but this proved to be a cumbersome and limited method of providing students with access to almost 500 links to resources in English and in Religious and Moral Education (RME). Another factor was that the use of sites previously evaluated by the teachers and the school librarian was seen to be of more value for many students, especially at the lower age end of the school, than the use of search engines. Many students found that the amount of material retrieved by search engines was both daunting and confusing, often commenting on the irrelevance of material found. The school

Earth Forces Website

Project Information

This web page has special links to a page on planning and to some previous examples.

You will be given two weeks during class time to produce a project about **Earthquakes and/or Volcanoes**. Much of this will be done in the school library but you will also need to spend time on your project outwith the Geography periods, possibly at home.

You will be using a range of resources (books, encyclopaedias, magazines, CD-ROMs, and the Internet) in the school but you can also use materials which you may have at home.

Aim: Using the resources, write a project (minimum of 2 sides of A4 paper, no maximum!) on **earthquakes and/or volcanoes**.

Ideas: Why, how and where earthquakes and/or volcanoes occur; how they are measured and predicted; what is done to prepare for these natural disasters; actual case studies of these hazards.

Your work will be **assessed** according to the following elements:

- Planning – more help is available with this on the planning page.
- Collecting Evidence
- Recording and Presenting
- Interpreting and Evaluating.

Each element is worth **5 marks**, giving a total of **20 marks**. See your teacher for more information about how your project will be marked.

Advice:
- keep a note of all of the resources you use – you'll need it for your bibliography.
- don't just hand in pages of printouts.....process this information!
- title all maps, diagrams, etc. and refer to these in your writing.
- use your own words at all times.
- read over your account before you hand it in and correct any mistakes.

Try to do the best you can...and enjoy doing your project!

 Linlithgow Academy Geography Department

Figure 8.9 Project outline for students at Linlithgow Academy, Scotland, UK

Earth Forces Website

Planning

This page will help you to plan your project. You might find it helpful to **print** this page and **answer** the questions. You can then submit your completed version with your project as evidence of planning.

Decide on what you want to research – (earthquakes **and/or** volcanoes).

Complete: I want to investigate_____.

Decide on relevant headings or aims in an order that makes sense. Try to ask some 'why' questions as these will help you to get more marks for explaining things later. Think of at least 5 headings/questions. **Complete**:

1._____

2._____

3._____

4._____

5._____

Put a tick beside the ways you will try to present information:

- tables
- graphs
- maps
- diagrams
- photographs.

Try to present your information in at least **three** different ways other than text. Keep a note of the resources you use for your **bibliography** (list of resources).

Linlithgow Academy Geography Department

Figure 8.10 Information skills advice for students at Linlithgow Academy, Scotland, UK

librarian discussed the site content with the teachers and designed the site, with the teachers providing appropriate text in relation to the topics covered. The school librarian is fortunate in having a parent helper who does searches for topics and identifies potential sites which are then evaluated by the teachers and the school librarian.

In an interview with the author, the school librarian identified the following benefits of the site:

- The site can be used by several classes at once, with some students in class, some in the library and some in a computer classroom.
- Students in different subjects often require similar information, e.g. topics such as fox hunting can be the subject of a student's English discursive essay or an RME project.
- Students perceive the site as more attractive than a worksheet and it can be updated quickly, at no cost, and with no teacher time wasted photocopying sheets.
- Pupils who are reluctant learners are often more motivated when using computers, and use the site constructively.
- Co-operation with teachers combines professional skills in the school and leads to more use of print and electronic sources by students and teachers.
- The profile of the school library is enhanced when the school librarian contributes to ICT development amongst teachers as well as providing evaluated sources for teachers to use.

The Issues instructional website has a number of features; Figure 8.11 demonstrates how students are encouraged to think carefully about choosing a topic.

Students can gain access to a range of mediated websites and Figure 8.12 shows an example of resources provided for students on the topic of animal rights.

While the use of the Issues website has not been formally evaluated by the teachers and the school librarian, teachers have noted an improvement in the way students structure their work and the school librarian has seen an improvement in the way in which students approach learning resources. The use of the Issues website has thus been of benefit to students, who now pay closer attention to reading, note-taking and essay structure; to teachers, who are able to advise students on how to tackle an assignment and can encourage them to use the mediated websites; and to the school librarian, who provides

Discursive Essays

Argumentative and Discursive/Persuasive Writing

What you have to do.
You are being asked to consider a topic that is (hopefully) of general interest, to discuss your own opinions on the subject and to make clear your reasons for believing as you do. You do not have to "make anything up" as, for example, you have to do for a short story or even a description; therefore for the logical, scientific thinker a discursive essay is often a wise choice.

All you have to do is:
1. Choose a topic with which you are as familiar as possible and decide what you think about it. (You need not always have strong feelings on a subject; you can weigh up both sides of the argument from a neutral standpoint.)
2. Construct your argument in a reasonable and logical way, using vocabulary suitable for your purpose. ('It is because it is because I say so.' is not enough!)

Some basic rules.
Even if you have some knowledge of a given topic and definite opinions on it, you still have to be able to convince your reader that your ideas are both reasonable and sensible. In order to do this, you should consider your argument with the following points in mind. You must:
1. Choose your words and expressions so that you sound convincing without being too hysterical and one-sided.
2. Make sure that what you are saying is logical and acceptable.
3. Back up your opinion with as many reasons and examples as you can.
4. Build your case so that it is easily followed and not too jumbled and disjointed.

Summary
We can now sum up the dangers to be avoided:
1. Lack of knowledge of and interest in the subject.
2. Disorganisation.
3. Direct abuse.
4. Illogical leaps.
5. Sweeping generalisations.

Figure 8.11 Advice for students studying English at Linlithgow Academy, Scotland, UK

Animal Rights

Animal Rights – can experiments on animals be justified?

Why do we as a civilized society conduct experiments using animals? Experiments on animals fall into two main categories. Medical experiments which for example test the effectiveness of new drugs and safety testing which tries to establish whether substances and products such as cosmetics are harmful. Strict animal welfare laws control the use of laboratory animals in this country and the go ahead is only given for experiments if no alternative method is available and that any suffering and distress is kept to a minimum. Without experiments on animals, it is argued that it would be far harder to find cures for dangerous illnesses or discover if products are safe for humans to use.

Critics of animal experiments claim that over 100 million animals suffer and die throughout the world each year as a result of experiments, most without the benefit of any form of anaesthetic. Animals which do not die during an experiment, may be killed later so that they can be examined. Unlike human volunteers, who can choose to take part in medical tests, animals have no such option. How useful are experiments on animals anyway ? Animals are not that similar to humans and every year, drugs which were successfully tested on animals have to be withdrawn because they have unexpected side effects on humans.

Is it time to put an end to all animal experiments or is it an essential method of research ?

Related topics: Bloodsports, Endangered species, Factory farming, Fur trade, Zoos

*   http://learn.co.uk/yvote/debates/debates7.htm
    A short essay explaining why animals are important for medical research
*   http://learn.co.uk/yvote/debates/debates8.htm
    A short essay arguing against the use of animals in experiments
*   www.cofe.anglican.org/view/index.html
    The Church of England's view on animal rights
*   www.debatabase.org/details.asp?topicID=7
    The pros and cons of experimenting on animals
*   http://re-xs.ucsm.ac.uk/ethics/animal_rights.html
    The ethics and moral issues relating to animal welfare are looked at through a number of links from this site for schools
*   www.veganism.com/arpage.htm
    This site looks at frequently asked questions on animal welfare from the point of view of veganism

Issues

Figure 8.12   Resources about animal rights for students at Linlithgow Academy, Scotland, UK

an added value service and sees more and better use of learning resources in the library and in the school in general.

This case study has demonstrated some of the benefits of professional collaboration in a secondary/high school. Other schools can learn from this approach by identifying different professionals' skills in the areas of website development, subject knowledge and knowledge of resources, and combining these skills in a collaborative effort which will lead to improved student access to resources and student learning.

Filamentality

Filamentality is a feature of the Blue Web'n subject gateway (discussed above in Chapter 4). It allows teachers and school librarians to create simple yet very effective instructional websites which can be used by students who need access to mediated web resources. Filamentality has been used by many schools across the world and examples can be accessed via the Blue Web'n site at www. kn.pacbell.com/wired/fil. The example featured in Figure 8.13 was created by the School Librarian and Head of Science at Dixons City Technology College, England. The advantages of using Filamentality are identified by the School Librarian, Lynn Barrett:

* It can present students with a clear structure for a project.
* It provides students with links to websites mediated by the teacher and the school librarian, which the students can access online.
* Student motivation is increased as the projects can deal with topical issues.
* Student engagement is high and student debate is active.
* It is not a time-consuming task for the teacher and school librarian.

The topic chosen for the year 9 (12 to 13-year-old) students was Foot and Mouth Disease and the key issue was whether vaccination of animals should be used as a means to control the disease.

The student use of this resource proved to be very successful in the school and both teachers and the school librarian were encouraged by the way the students were stimulated by use of such a tool.

Hunt for FMD and Vaccination
an Internet Treasure Hunt on Immunisation

created by Lynn Barrett
Dixons CTC

Introduction | The Questions | Internet Resources

Introduction

In this Hunt you will use the Internet sites below and Factiva, the online news database in the Library, to track down information about Foot and Mouth Disease and the issues surrounding vaccination. Look at the impact of FMD beyond the farming community and imagine yourself in a position of having to make some of the difficult decisions that faced businesses, scientists, veterinarians and politicians.

Questions

1. Can immunisation, or vaccination, be used to prevent Food and Mouth Disease?
2. Why was the decision made to slaughter so many animals?
3. How quickly did the disease spread? What countries were affected?
4. Who was affected by Foot and Mouth Disease besides the farmers? What was the impact on the countryside?

The Internet Resources

- Questions and Answers on Foot and Mouth Disease (FMD)
- The Ramblers' Association: Foot and Mouth Disease
- The Issues Explained: Vaccination
- Foot and Mouth: Tracing the Epidemic

The Big Question

In the event of a future outbreak of Foot and Mouth Disease, should vaccination be used along with, or instead of, culling? If you are not a farmer, how might it affect you, and why is it important for you to have an informed opinion? How can you become informed?

Created by SBC's
Filamentality

Content by Lynn Barrett, lynn@dixonsctc.org.uk
www.kn.pacbell.com/wired/fil/pages/huntimmunisaly.html
Last revised Fri Jun 21 2:33:48 US/Pacific 2002

Figure 8.13   Use of Filamentality for year 9 students at Dixons City Technology College, West Yorkshire, UK (www.kn.pacbell.com/wired/fil/pages/huntimmunisaly.html)

WebQuests

Another form of instructional website that can be designed by teachers and school librarians who do not necessarily have web design skills takes the form of a WebQuest. March (1998) argues that the advantages of using WebQuests include:

- Students can be more motivated when given a problem-solving exercise based on real-world events.
- Students' thinking skills are enhanced: 'First, the question posed to students can not be answered simply by collecting and spitting back information. A WebQuest forces students to transform information into something else: a cluster that maps out the main issues, a comparison, a hypothesis, a solution, etc.'
- Students can work co-operatively on WebQuests and can develop new skills not only in using the web but in developing arguments and sharing tasks.
- WebQuests can be used in schools even where computer resources are scarce.

Figure 8.14 shows the key elements of a WebQuest for teachers and school librarians about to design a WebQuest. Figure 8.15 shows part of a WebQuest designed for geography students at St Joseph's College, Australia.

Thus it can be seen that WebQuests are similar in design to Filamentality and that both focus clearly on encouraging students to examine sometimes complex issues but providing them with scaffolding which guides them to key questions and evaluated resources.

Conclusion

There is no doubt that the use of instructional websites in schools will develop greatly in the next few years as teachers and school librarians learn more ICT skills in relation to website development, but it is also clear that the use of Filamentality and WebQuests provide teachers and school librarians with easily designed but very effective instructional websites which their students can use.

WebQuests
for learning

Designing for Success

Use the Designer's Checklist below once you think you're ready
to create your WebQuest. If you feel like you could use any
tips on particular aspects of your potential WebQuest, click in
the matching checkboxes for a few friendly suggestions.

☐ An Engaging Opening

☐ The Question / Task

☐ Background for Everyone

☐ Roles / Expertise

☐ Use of the Web

☐ Transformative Thinking

☐ Real World Feedback

☐ Conclusion

Your Name: _____

How About Some Friendly Advice...

G'Day!   freebies   the ozline story   bald self-promotion   site sorter   good-bye!

Figure 8.14   Guide to designing WebQuests (www.ozline.com/webquests/checklist.html)

Touring Antarctica

An Internet WebQuest on Antarctica
created by Camilla Elliott St Joseph's College – Mildura

Introduction | The Task | The Process & Resources | Conclusion | Teachers

Introduction
Antarctica is one of the last unspoilt environments on Earth, relatively untouched
by humans. As modern technology permits more and more people to visit this
beautiful wilderness, the risk of damage and pollution becomes an increasing
threat. Can we afford the costs of increased human activity in Antarctica? In this
class you will work in teams to establish the environmental impact of increased
tourism in Antarctica from the point of view of a number of interest groups and
present your conclusion as to whether or not this planned tour should be permitted
to go ahead.

The Quest
A new tourist company, 'Antarctic Tours', wants to establish monthly trekking
tours in the Antarctic for four months from November to the end of February.
They plan to take 400 trekkers to Antarctica during this four months each year.
The Australian government has requested that an Environmental Impact Team
explore the impact of this tourism proposal on the animals and natural
environment of Antarctica. The Environmental Impact Team will be made up of a
Tour Operator, an Environmentalist, a Scientist and a Politician. This Team will
present a report to the government with recommendations to either support or
argue against giving the go ahead for 'Antarctic Tours' to begin operations in
November this year.

The report must be supported with factual information relating to each interest
group and present a valid argument to support the views of all stakeholders. The
completed report will be presented to Australian government representatives and
be used to decide if the venture is to be allowed to go ahead.

The Process and Resources
In this WebQuest you will be working together in groups. You will use the
webpages that have been provided but may also use general book resources from
the library collection. Each group will consist of eight (8) students who will divide
into pairs and take on one of the roles of either Tour Operator, Environmentalist,
Scientist or Politician and complete the quest task.

Once each pair has researched and developed an Environmental Impact
Statement in relation to their role, they will come together as a group to develop a
conclusion and recommendation to be presented to the government on behalf of
the whole team.

Figure 8.15 WebQuest for students at St Joseph's College, Australia

References

Bafile, C. (2002) Physics with 'FIZZ', *Education World*,
www.education-world.com/a_curr/webwizard075.shtml.

Community High School District 99 (2003) *Designing Teacher Websites*,
www.csd99.k12.il.us/north/library/PDF/frontpage.pdf.

Gardner, D. (2003) *Tips for Developing the Geography Department Website*,
www.raincliffe.com.

March, T. (1998) *Why WebQuests?*, www.ozline.com/webquests/intro.html.

McKenzie, J. (2002) *Beyond Technology*, Bellingham, WA, FNO Press.

Moore, A. (2001) Designing for the Web, *Teaching History Online*, (5) (April),
www.spartacus.schoolnet.co.uk/history5a.htm.

9

Future developments

After reading this chapter, you will be able to:

- evaluate future trends in the curriculum
- critically examine future trends in the internet for schools
- evaluate the implications of the above trends for the teaching and learning of information skills in schools
- critically examine the future role of the teacher and the school librarian.

Introduction

The developments in ICT have been dramatic in the past few years and there have been many changes within schools in relation to the curriculum. Teachers and school librarians in many countries complain of being overloaded with changes and being unable to cope with them. Change is a constant factor in today's schools and this change is likely to continue. This chapter seeks to examine some of these possible changes in relation to future trends in the school curriculum, how new trends in the internet might affect schools, why teaching information skills is likely to be a key aspect of the future curriculum and how the roles of teachers and school librarians might change in the future.

The future curriculum

Hargreaves (2002) argues that the curriculum in UK schools must move forward to being a 'curriculum for learning' and that teaching in schools should develop into a 'pedagogy for learning'. Hargreaves also argues:

The goal is that students should know as much as before, be better than in the past at the basic skills of literacy and numeracy, and have new skills and competences, such as ICT skills, teamwork, managing one's own learning, creativity, entrepreneurship and enterprise. This can only be achieved by a new approach to learning, in which students learn faster and/or learn more than one thing at a time (a richer curriculum) at the hands of more skilful teachers (a better pedagogy) supported by a reformed approach to assessment (assessment for learning).

The curriculum of the future is as likely to be influenced by politicial decisions in different countries as it is today but it is clear that in most countries, the curriculum is designed to try to make students into better citizens and to make them suitable for the world of employment. The UK's Department for Education and Skills (DfES) (2002) argues that 'Every child, whatever their circumstances, requires an education that equips them for work and prepares them to succeed in the wider economy and in society' and that the future curriculum needs to cater for the individual needs of students. Increasingly, this means that future students need to become better at accessing information and using ICT than today's students, as there is likely to be more demand for knowledge workers in the future. The key skills of knowledge workers are not technical ones, but skills in identifying problems and issues and in seeking solutions through accessing key information resources and using these resources effectively.

Future trends in the internet

Changes in the efficency of technology such as faster PCs, increased bandwith and the development of more sophisticated mobile technology are likely to mean that more people across the world will have faster and better access to the internet. The Cordis Advisory Group (2003) argues that the two key developments in the internet are likely to be, first, the 'High Performance Internet', which will provide universities and schools with improved networking, allowing them to make better use of distance learning, and access to vast databases of information across the world. The implications for schools are, first, that future students will be able to access sites with large video content without having bandwith problems and, second, that learning from home may be an option for senior students. The second development identified by the Cordis Advisory Group is the 'Commodity Internet', which refers to the use of the internet in the home, often for leisure purposes such as home shopping or web-based games. The group argues:

> High-performance Internet developments today, whether undertaken in Europe or the USA, will feed through into future products exploiting higher speeds, more advanced switches, and better protocols, which will form the basis of the commodity Internet in a few years time.

The implications for schools are that both parents and students are likely to have much better internet access from home and will be able to access the school's website or intranet (password-protected) which will contain much more multimedia information than at present. Clearly, schools will have to consider how they should make the best use of the internet for teaching; one outcome may be that students will be able to access much more of the curriculum online than at present. Thus, teachers and school librarians are likely to come under pressure from school managers to develop more online learning and more access to mediated online learning resources.

Implications for teaching information skills

Given the above developments, it is clear that the importance of teaching information skills to students in both secondary/high schools and in primary/elementary schools is not likely to diminish. Students will need more sophisticated information skills in the future as they are faced with more multimedia information in the form of websites with a mixture of text, graphics and photographs – as at present – but also with a larger element of video and simulation material. The need for improved skills in 'reading' these sites will be a challenge for teachers and school librarians who themselves have been accustomed to more text and graphics-based sites. The key areas of Purpose, Location, Use and Self-evaluation will still be important in the future but the teaching of skills will have to be geared to students' needs, particularly in the area of interpreting and evaluating increasingly sophisticated websites. The need for students to be able to evaluate the content of future web-based material will be greater than it is today because the delivery of the messages on the web, some of which are designed to mislead and not to inform, will be more sophisticated and it will be harder for students to identify the misleading aspects of very well designed sites.

Future students are also likely to be presenting their project work using more sophisticated means. However, the fact that students will be able to include in their presentations web-like aspects, such as links to resources, photographs and video, does not mean that the *quality* of the students' work will increase. Unless future students can use their information skills to use information effectively and to organize their findings well, they may present teachers with projects that use advanced design skills but lack focus or depth. Teachers and school librarians will need to ensure that students understand that their use of argument and a logical structure are much more important than the use of advanced design skills.

Future roles of the teacher and the school librarian

Dowling (2003) argues that while there will be an increase in the use of what she terms 'pedagogical agents' such as online learning packages, the role of the teacher as a human contact for students is likely to be important although the role is likely to change over time. While future teachers will increasingly use computer-based learning packages and web-based materials, Dowling states that:

> It can also be argued that the human teacher is in a strong position, in particular by virtue of overall life experience and sophistication as a communicator, to both model and facilitate co-operative learning behaviours. And who better than a 'real' teacher to recognise and develop 'authentic' contexts for learning?

The role of the teacher in the future will be less that of an instructor and more that of a facilitator who can guide students and help them to become more independent learners. However, this does not mean that the teacher will have less work to do. Rather, teachers will be faced with *more* demanding challenges in designing meaningful learning experiences for their students; this will mean that teachers will have to develop new skills in areas such as curriculum design as well as instructional website design.

The future role of the school librarian will also reflect changes in the future curriculum and in technology. Herring (2000) argues that the future role will include three aspects: educator, information manager and expert adviser. As future educators, school librarians will play a key role in meeting the information skills needs of both teachers and students. As information managers, school librarians will ensure that schools benefit from the web development outlined above, so that a school's access to broadband web resources will be developed by school librarians to allow students and teachers greater access to enhanced learning resources. As expert advisers, school librarians will play a key role as intranet developers and will train teachers to use online sources more effectively in the curriculum and to design instructional websites which incorporate information skills guidance as well as access to online resources.

One key factor will be increased co-operation between the teacher and the school librarian, who will need to use each other's professional skills to cope with the demands of the future curriculum and future students. The combination of the teacher's subject knowledge and the school librarian's knowledge of learning resources, both print and online, and of web design skills, will be needed to provide students with adequate support.

Conclusion

The school of the future may be physically different from today's schools and school students will not necessarily attend school every day as they do at present. Online learning is likely to be much more common in schools in the future and the success of both face-to-face and online learning will depend on the ability of teachers and school librarians to adapt to new technologies, new curricula, new and more sophisticated online resources and new methods of delivery. Learning will remain the key focus for schools: learning skills, including information skills, will be of prime importance in tomorrow's schools.

References

Cordis Advisory Group (2003) *The Future of the Internet*, www.cordis.lu/esprit/src/i2eurepo.htm.

Department for Education and Skills (2002) *Schools – Achieving Success*, London, DfES, www.dfes.gov.uk/achievingsuccess/index.shtml.

Dowling, C. (2003) *The Role of the Human Teacher in Learning Environments of the Future*, Australian Computer Society, http://crpit.com/confpapers/CRPITV23Dowling.pdf.

Hargreaves, D. (2002) *A Future for the School Curriculum*, www.qca.org.uk/ca/14-19/dh_speech.asp.

Herring, J. (2000) The 21st Century School Librarian: educator, information manager and expert adviser, *Impact*, 3 (6) June, www.careerdevelopmentgroup.org.uk/impact/0600/herringJ.htm.

Bibliography

AASL/AECT (1998) *Information Power: building partnerships for learning*, Chicago, IL, ALA.

Bafile, C. (2002) Physics with 'FIZZ', *Education World*, www.education-world.com/a_curr/webwizard075.shtml.

Barrett, L. and Danks, M. (2003) Information Literacy: a crucial role for schools, *Library & Information Update*, **2** (5) (May), 42–4.

Becta (2002) *Designing Effective Websites*, www.becta.org.uk.

Becta (2003) *Common Factors in Successful ICT Practice*, www.ictadvice.org.uk/index.php.

Bellingham Public Schools (2003) *Designing School Homepages*, www.bham.wednet.edu/technology/webrules.htm.

Bradley, P. (2002) *The Advanced Internet Searcher's Handbook*, 2nd edn, London, Library Association Publishing [3rd edn, 2004, Facet Publishing].

Carnell, E. and Lodge, C. (2002) *Supporting Effective Learning*, London, Paul Chapman.

Carter, M. (2002) The Connecting School and the Intranet Librarian, *School Libraries Worldwide*, **8** (2) (July), 51–64.

College of New Caledonia Library (2003) *Evaluating Websites – questions to ask*, www.cnc.bc.ca/library/evaluatingwebsites.html.

Community High School District 99 (2003) *Designing Teacher Websites*, www.csd99.k12.il.us/north/library/PDF/frontpage.pdf.

Conlon, T. (2002) Information Mapping as a Support for Learning and Teaching, *Computer Education*, (102) (November), 2–12.

Cordis Advisory Group (2003) *The Future of the Internet*, www.cordis.lu/esprit/src/i2eurepo.htm.

Department for Education and Skills (2002) *Schools – Achieving Success*, London, DfES, www.dfes.gov.uk/achievingsuccess/index.shtml.

Department for Education and Skills (2003) *Fulfilling the Potential*, London, DfES.

Dowling, C. (2003) *The Role of the Human Teacher in Learning Environments of the Future*, Australian Computer Society, http://crpit.com/confpapers/CRPITV23.Dowling.pdf.

Doyle, C. (1994) *Information Literacy in an Information Society*, ERIC Clearing House on Information and Technology.

ED's Oasis (2003) *Web Site Evaluation for Educators*, www.classroom.com/edsoasis.

Eisenberg, M. and Berkowitz, R. (1988) *Information Problem Solving: the Big Six approach to library and information skills instruction*, Ablex, www.big6.com.

Fryer, A. (2003) *Writing Webpages with Wesley*, www.wtvi.com/html/handout.html.

Gardner, D. (2003) *Tips for Developing the Geography Department Website*, www.raincliffe.com.

Gibson, S., Oberg, D. and Peltz, R. (1999) *Internet Use in Alberta Schools: a multiphase study*, www.carleton.ca/amtec99/Internet-Alberta.doc.

Grover, R., Fox, C. and Lakin, J. McC. (eds) (2001) *The Handy 5*, Lanham, MD, Scarecrow Press.

Hains, A. (2002) *Considerations for Website Users*, www.uwm.edu/~annhains/appendix_b.htm.

Hargreaves, D. (2002) *A Future for the School Curriculum*, www.qca.org.uk/ca/14-19/dh_speech.asp.

Herring, J. (1996) *Teaching Information Skills in Schools*, London, Library Assocation Publishing.

Herring, J., Tarter, A.-M. and Naylor, S. (2000) Theory into Practice: using the PLUS model to teach information skills and support the curricululum in a secondary school. In Howe, E. (2000) *Developing Information Literacy*, Spring, TX, LMC Source.

Herring, J., Tarter, A.-M. and Naylor, S. (2002) An Evaluation of the Use of the PLUS Model to Develop Pupils' Information Skills in a Secondary School, *School Libraries Worldwide*, **8** (1) (January), 1–24.

Hyerle, D. (2000) *A Field Guide to Using Visual Tools*, Lyme, NH, Association for Supervision and Curriculum Development.

Ictadvice (2003) *What are the Management Issues of Teacher Access to the Web and Email?*, www.ictadvice.org.uk.

Kent Educational Authority (2003) *How will the Internet Enhance Learning?*, www.kented.org.uk/ngfl/policy/question4.html.

Kinchin, I. and Hay, D. (2000) How a Qualitative Approach to Concept Map Analysis can be Used to Aid Learning by Illustrating Patterns of Conceptual Development, *Educational Research*, **42** (1) (Spring), 43–57.

Kuhlthau, C. (1989) Information Search Process, *School Library Media Quarterly*, **22** (1) Fall, 19–25, www.scils.rutgers.edu/~kuhlthau/Search%20Process.htm.

Kyriacou, C. (1998) *Essential Teaching Skills*, 2nd edn, Cheltenham, Stanley Thornes.

Langford, L. (2000) Information Literacy? Seeking clarification. In Howe, E. (ed.), *Developing Information Literacy*, IASL/LMC Source.

Lerman, J. (1998) You've Got Mail!, *Electronic School Online*, www.electronic-school.com/0398f5.html.

Leu, D. (2002) Internet Workshop: making time for literacy, *The Reading Teacher*, (February), www.readingonline.org

Lieberman, D. (1999) *Learning: behaviour and cognition*, 3rd edn, Florence, KY, Wadsworth.

Loertscher, D. (2000) *Taxonomies of the School Library Media Program*, 2nd edn, Spring, TX, Hi Willow Research and Publishing.

Loertscher, D. and Woolls, B. (2002) *Information Literacy: a review of the research*, 2nd edn, Spring, TX, Hi Willow Research and Publishing.

March, T. (1998) *Why WebQuests?*, www.ozline.com/webquests/intro.html.

Matusevich, M. (1995) *School Reform – what role can technology play in a constructivist setting?*, http://pixel.cs.vt.edu/edu/fis/techcons.html.

McKenzie, J. (2000) *Beyond Technology: questioning, research and the information literate school*, Bellingham, WA, FNO Press.

McKenzie, J. (2003) *Home Sweet Home: creating WWW pages that deliver*, http://fno.org.

Moore, A. (2001) Designing for the Web, *Teaching History Online*, (5) (April), www.spartacus.schoolnet.co.uk/history5a.htm.

Netdays Australia (2000) *Cultural Journey into Australia*, http://netdays.edna.edu.au/2000.

Noodletools (2003) *Choose the Best Search for Your Information Need*, www.noodletools.com/debbie/literacies/information/5locate/adviceengine.html.

Northamptonshire County Council (2000) *Developing an Internet Access Policy for Your School*, www.northants-ecl.gov.uk/apps/ICT/dia/hme.asp.

Notess, G. (1999) *Definitions for Terminology Used*, www.searchengineshowdown.com/glossary.html.

November, A. (1998) *Teaching Zack to Think*, www.anovember.com/articles/zack.html.

Pedley, P., (2001) *The Invisible Web*, London, Aslib-IMI.

Robert Gordon University and Queen Margaret University College

(RGU/QMUC) (2001) *Library Support for ICT in the Curriculum: reader*, RGU/QMUC (available for purchase, contact cwhitehead@rgu.ac.uk).

Ryan, J. and Capra, S. (2001) Information Literacy Planning for Educators: the ILPO approach, *School Libraries Worldwide*, **7** (1) (January), 1–10, www.aber-ac.uk/tfpl/elibs/s/worldwide.asp.

Sandwell Education and Lifelong Learning (2002) *Schools Internet Access Policy*, www.lea.sandwell.gov.uk/lea/docs/schools-internet.pdf.

School Libraries on the Web (2003) *Search Engines*, www.sldirectory.com/searchf/engines.html#engines.

Schrock, K. (1999) *The ABCs of Website Evaluation*, http://school.discovery.com/schrockguide/pdf/weval.pdf

Schunk, D. (2000) *Learning Theories: an educational perspective*, 3rd edn, Upper Saddle River, NJ, Prentice Hall.

Slowinski, J. (1999) Internet in America's Schools, *First Monday*, **4** (1), www.firstmonday.dk/issues/issue4_1/slowinski/.

Smith, K. (2003) The Primary School Curriculum PLUS Information Skills Models, unpublished MSc dissertation, Queen Margaret University College, Edinburgh.

Stevens Institute of Technology (2003) *Alliance + Project*, http://k12science.ati.stevens-tech.edu/alliance/admin/resadm.html

Teachers Online Project (2003) *Case Studies*, http://top.ngfl.gov.uk .

Thomas, N. (1999) *Information Literacy and Information Skills Instruction*, Westport, CT, Libraries Unlimited.

Tileston, D. (2000) *10 Best Teaching Practices*, Thousand Oaks, CA, Corwin Press.

Todd, R. (2003) Learning in the Information Age School: opportunities, outcomes and options, Keynote Paper, International Association of School Librarianship (IASL) 2003 Annual Conference, Durban, South Africa, 7–11 July 2003, www.iasl-org/conference2003-virtual.html.

Trilling, B. and Hood, P. (2001) Learning Technology and Education Reform in the Knolwedge Age. In Paechter, C. et al., *Learning, Space and Identity*, London, Paul Chapman Publishing.

Tubbs, M. (1996) *The New Teacher*, London, David Fulton Publishers.

Valenza, J. (2001) *A Webquest about Evaluating Websites*, http://mciu.org/~spjvweb/evalwebstu.html.

Virtual Teacher Centre (2003) *Integrating ICT into History*, http://vtc.ngfl.gov.uk/docserver.php?temid=271.

Web Style Guide (2003), www.webstyleguide.com.

Index